TV Moms

TV Moms

mTV Moms

An Illustrated Guide

Ray Richmond

New York

Library of Congress Cataloging-in-Publication Data
Richmond, Ray.
  TV Moms / by Ray Richmond
    p. cm.
  ISBN 1-57500-130-6 (pbk.)
  1. Mothers on television. I. Title.
PN1992.8.M58 R53 2000
791.45'6520431—dc21
                                        00-029918

All photos courtesy of Photofest.

The publisher has made every effort to secure permission to reproduce copyrighted material and would like to apologize should there have been any errors or omissions.

TV Books, L.L.C.
1619 Broadway, Ninth Floor
New York, NY 10019
www.tvbooks.com

Interior design by Deborah Daly
MANUFACTURED IN THE UNITED STATES OF AMERICA

Contents

* Dates refer to the years during which a particular actress played the
  role.

Introduction

Telemothering: The First Fifty Years

They have indirectly held our hands, treated our injuries, baked us cookies, guided us through the minefield of childhood, adolescence, and adulthood. They have taught us how to ward off bullies and fight a cold, helped answer our various and sundry questions about life and showed us compassion by example. They have, in short, instructed many of us in the fine art of being human.

They are moms. And not just any moms, of course, but the best kind: TV moms.

In the fifty years they have inhabited America's living rooms, mother characters on television have touched us, inspired us, amused us, infuriated us, and entertained us in ways that transcend mere flickering images housed inside an electronic gadget.

This book aims to illustrate exactly how the fifty-plus mothers profiled herein—presiding on shows airing from the 1950s through the present day—have grown to become fixtures as familiar to us (and often as beloved) as members of our own families.

And it's no wonder that the nation has consistently embraced these women as it has few others in the entertainment world. Real moms have emulated them. The rest of America enjoys a kinship with them. TV moms have often proven more dependable in many ways then even our own mothers. They never punished us, or rejected us, or disappointed us, or left us feeling angry, sad, frightened, or insecure. They loved us unconditionally and asked nothing in return save for a weekly half-hour of our lives, which we were only too happy to grant them.

In the early days of television, mother characters personified omnipotent creatures blessed with oodles of patience, sincerity, energy, and love. They have changed markedly in the course of roughly fifty years dating to the dawn of TV in the late 1940s and early '50s. In their first incarnation, TV moms emerged as Eisenhower-era creatures who were expected to keep their waistlines impossibly trim and have dinner piping hot on the table when dad/hubby stumbled exhaustedly through the door.

The TV mothering approach fostered by Lucy Ricardo, Harriet Nelson, Margaret Anderson, June Cleaver, and Donna Stone served to define the maternal style and principles of a generation. They supplied reason and soothing reassurance, keeping their heads while all of those around them were losing theirs. Innocent warmth and homespun family values were the fuel that kept the telemothering fires burning.

At the same time, those first telemom pioneers existed as doting household slaves content to serve—and always with a smile. Before the 1960s were through, one Carol Brady scooted onto the TV scene, carrying a promise that the milk-and-cookies era of the TV mom would continue into the 1970s unabated. But while Carol never wavered an inch from her sunny view of life, the world around her soon changed a bit for the grittier.

Indeed, the early image of TV momhood invariably evolved into the seeming reality denial of the '70s via the likes of the Waltons, the Bradys, and the Partridges. Their motherly heroines all had a way of holding a messier reality at apron-string's length (even if Shirley Partridge never really wore one), obscured as it was beneath a certain glossy, see-yourself-in-the-shine sheen. But the TV audience accepted it without much squawking, because it represented an idealized version of American family life that the nation could never quite achieve but to which it always aspired.

This trend was fought, however, and eventually transformed by breakthrough shows like *All in the Family* and *Maude*, which creator-producer Norman Lear used to pierce many of TV's longstanding barriers that blocked many social issues and coarse language. Lear's influence on situation comedy was enormous, and his depiction of TV moms (and dads and kids) went farther than anyone in closing the gap between TV land and the real world.

By the 1980s and then into the '90s, moms of every stripe would be jumping out of our television sets: white-collar moms (Clair Huxtable on *The Cosby Show)*, blue-collar moms (Roseanne Conner on *Roseanne*), neurotic moms (Jamie Buchman of *Mad About You*), loudmouth moms (Sophia Petrillo on *The Golden Girls*), impossibly together moms (Annie Camden of the WB's *7th Heaven*), henpecking, shop-a-moms (Peg Bundy on *Married...With Children*), sassy moms (Jill Taylor on *Home Improvement*), conflicted moms (Elyse Keaton on *Family Ties*), menopausal moms (Cybill Sheridan on *Cybill*), clueless moms (Estelle Costanza of *Seinfeld*), denial-fueled moms (Mrs. Cartman on *South Park*), happily single moms (Murphy Brown on *Murphy Brown*), even nurturing moms with blue beehive hair (Marge Simpson on *The Simpsons*).

TV moms have matured to showcase engagingly diverse personalities. An eclectic bunch, they no longer simply take orders and suffer silently; today, they give as good as they get (sometimes better). The empowerment and independence that were painfully missing from maternal characterizations on the tube in the 1950s and early '60s have long since been plugged into the primetime consciousness.

So it has all come full circle for the TV mom. At the outset, our primetime mothers required nothing more than the devotion of their families and an occa-sional pat on the rear. These days, they demand at least as much nurturing as they dispense. They have learned that the one-way street is a dead end, so they carry friends outside of the marriage, jobs outside of the home and, on occasion, even feelings outside of their understanding. They are smarter, funnier, more savvy, more versatile, and decidedly more high-maintenance than they have ever been.

While there is an acknowledgment in today's primetime TV environment that moms come in all shapes and sizes, attitudes, marital statuses, and social strata, this has not necessarily included women of all colors and ethnicities. Mothers on TV have successfully progressed from their lily-white roots via the likes of Julia Baker (*Julia*), Florida Evans (*Good Times*), Louise Jefferson (*The Jeffersons*), and of course Mrs. Huxtable as well as more contemporary characters including Dee Mitchell (UPN's *Moesha*). Even so, it speaks volumes that while the tube has managed to give us a memorable mom who happened to be an automobile (*My Mother the Car*), it has yet to serve up a strong ma of Latino or Asian ancestry. Even African-American mothers were essentially invisible until twenty years after television's formal commercial launch, when Diahann Carroll was cast as the tube's first high-profile black mom in 1968 with *Julia*.

To be sure, the plight and belief system of the TV mom has more or less mirrored that of society itself. She and her brethren aren't just good for baking a mean apple pie. They have even been known of late to endure bouts of depression, undergo abortions, question their lot in life, and—(gasp)—even have an affair once in a while. The sense of make-believe that once colored a TV mom's existence has, over the years, been honed into a decidedly more realistic edge.

A few years ago, an episode of a gritty Fox drama series entitled *413 Hope Street* opened with a sixteen-year-old mother carrying her infant into a youth crisis center. She explains that she was "lookin' to get some food" for her baby. The mother is then interviewed by a counselor who asks, "Have you been tested for HIV? Are you on any drugs? Have you worked as a prostitute? Is your boyfriend this baby's father?"

Is this more reflective of the real world than was the pristine domain once populated by Margaret and June? Undoubtedly. Is it more educational? Absolutely. Is it healthier to watch? Not necessarily.

And yet even in such dire circumstances the importance of mother in the familial structure is never questioned. Fathers can often be ignorant and oafish (or absent) inside the nuclear and post-nuclear home of the TV age, but moms rarely are. They continue to be the straw that stirs the nightly drink we call network TV—only today, they can mix it in a multitude of ways.

So it will be reflected in *TV Moms*, a book that aims—in its own small way—to stand not merely as a celebration of tele-motherhood but a genuine assessment of how it has impacted our lives. If it seems a somewhat wacky notion to attach such importance onto fictitious characters spouting the lines of staff writers, well, let's just say it wouldn't feel that way to anyone who ever watched June serve dinner to Ward, Wally, and the Beav.

—Ray Richmond

~1~

The 1950s and '60s
I Am Mother,
Hear Me Serve

*I*n the beginning, there was *Lucy*. Well, actually, that isn't entirely true. There was Mary Kay Stearns of *Mary Kay and Johnny*—and then there was Lucy. Lucy begot Harriet Nelson, who begot Margaret Anderson, who begot June Cleaver, Ruth Martin, and Donna Stone, as well as an image of motherhood and family that was steeped in glorious fantasy.

The initial appearance of the TV mom can be pegged to December 19, 1948, on a pioneering situation comedy called *Mary Kay and Johnny*. The Johnny was Mary Kay's real-life husband, Johnny Stearns. Their series had been on the air little more than a year when the fateful night arrived.

In an early example of art aping reality, the actual Mary Kay gave birth to a son, Christopher, a mere thirty minutes before airtime. That evening, those few American households that owned a TV set (perhaps fifty thousand in '48) saw Johnny Stearns perform solo on the show in the role of an expectant father pacing the maternity ward. He would get word just as the episode concluded: he was now a daddy—both on TV and off.

Then something happened that would never fly at all today: the Stearns' real son Chris was added to the show's cast less than a month after his birth, appearing in his bassinet. Thus, Mary Kay Stearns was able to showcase her actual mothering skills on national TV, parenting her actual boy. It was weird, but it was still the late '40s, and frankly no one knew any better.

That seemingly invasive, quasi-real approach would spread to other, far more familiar, pioneering family comedies on the tube. As we all know, Lucille Ball and her real-life husband, Desi Arnaz, made TV history together in the 1950s as the fictionalized couple Lucy and Ricky Ricardo on *I Love Lucy*. And the Stearns' TV parenting served as a mere prelude to the most intensive buildup to a birth in the medium's history: that of Little Ricky on *I Love Lucy* on January 19, 1953.

What proved a bit remarkable was the fact that the *Lucy* baby episode aired the same night that the real Lucy was giving birth to her second child, Desi Jr. It was the sort of uncanny coincidence that viewers of the era craved.

Right about that same time, a third TV family appeared on the scene to blur the line separating fantasy and reality still further. *The Adventures of Ozzie & Harriet* arrived in 1952 and stuck around for a whopping fourteen seasons, starring Ozzie and Harriet Nelson and their sons, David and Ricky. The most intriguing thing about the show was that not only did this family portray the Nelsons on television, they were the Nelsons, period—a genuine family depicting a doggedly sanitized version of itself for America. The Nelsons even lived in a TV home modeled after their real-life house in Hollywood.

Despite the overwhelming success of *I Love Lucy* and *Ozzie & Harriet*, however, the ersatz-realism gambit quickly became more of a limited novelty than a genuine ongoing trend. What remained intact throughout the 1950s and '60s, however, was a TV view of motherhood that kept a safe distance from any honest scrutiny in assessing the true challenges of raising kids.

And to be sure, the carefully cultivated image of the early TV mom (the Cro-Momnan period, if you will) carried with it some authentic fallout. For instance, any kid who watched *I Love Lucy*, *Leave It to Beaver*, and *Ozzie & Harriet* had to wonder if babies really did arrive by stork.

The couples never slept in the same bed; their relationships seemed chaste save for the occasional light embrace and peck in the general region of one another's lips. Even when pregnant, TV moms through the late 1960s were unable to utter the word "pregnant" on the air. It was considered too racy even to imply that husbands and wives engaged in coital splendor for the sake of procreation. Advertisers believed that women demanded a sparkling clean television environment, and so that's what they would get until further notice.

TV's first maternal icons were idealized creations who perfectly matched the innocent social optimism and isolation of the early postwar era. They were cheerful but studious, easygoing yet firm. They were in charge in a strong-yet-feminine way. On the rare occasion when their emotions ran out of whack, it was dismissed as uncharacteristic and rather adorable. These were, after all, women without evident flaws.

Not that they couldn't occasionally be nags. That became particularly true as the 1960s developed and Laura Petrie (Mary Tyler Moore) was often shown to be a high-octane handful for her husband Rob (Dick Van Dyke) on *The Dick Van Dyke Show*. But the rule clear through the early 1970s was that mothers—even the semi-ghoulish Morticia Addams (Carolyn Jones) on *The Addams Family* and Lily Munster on *The Munsters*—were held up as essentially wholesome, middle-class, sensible, and unfailingly all-American.

The moms of TV's first twenty years were wired to make the world feel safe for everyone around them. And that's pretty much what they did, even on the off chance they happened to be witches (Samantha Stephens on *Bewitched*), automobiles (the 1928 Porter on *My Mother the Car*), or animated creations (Wilma Flintstone and Betty Rubble on *The Flintstones*). They provided a sheltered, pristine haven that was practically an embodiment of the womb itself.

Sexiness did not figure into the motherly mix until much later on. These moms were way too busy being pillars of wisdom and support to acknowledge that part of themselves. Ironically, one of the first TV moms to exhibit anything resembling a libido—and who seemed comfortable with being both sex object and mother figure—was the monsterly Morticia in *The Addams Family*. She would wear those slinky black gowns and spout something in French. Gomez (John Astin) would go a little nuts with desire. But the message was that it was all right because these weren't really people, anyway.

In hindsight, the restrictive decrees of yore appear pretty absurd to us today. But in truth they didn't seem to bother anyone all that much back then. And in spite of their decidedly reality-challenged behavior, mothers like Harriet and June were celebrated as national treasures all the same.

Lucy Ricardo
(Lucille Ball)

I Love Lucy
(Oct. 15, 1951 to June 14, 1957), CBS

When we think of Lucy Ricardo, few of us flash on a nurturing mother rocking a bassinet. We instead envision a wacky redhead hawking the alcohol-based health tonic Vitameatavegamin on TV and getting drunk on the air. We think of a wife trying to crash her husband's nightclub act, or a crazy dame fighting in a vat of unpressed grapes, or struggling to wrap chocolates on a speedy factory conveyer belt—or prying loose John Wayne's footprints from in front of the Grauman's Chinese Theatre.

But Lucy was a mom, all right. In fact, her January 19, 1953 birth of Little Ricky was the highest-rated single episode of television in the 1950s. That the show aired the same night on which Lucille Ball herself brought son Desi Arnaz, Jr., into the world made it all the more special. It was art imitating life, TV comedy-style.

Until the final season of *I Love Lucy* (1956–57), Lucy's telemothering skills were essentially restricted to using a largely-unseen baby as comic fodder. She would be stressed out trying to quell Little Ricky's crying, for the most part. Then in the show's last year, a child actor named Richard Keith was added to the cast as the now five-year-old boy. And his role was mostly to inspire various forms of bedlam in the Ricardo apartment.

As a mom, Lucy followed the early TV example of the June Cleavers, the Donna Stones, and the Harriet Nelsons. They were all loving and lovely, wholesome white women who were seldom touched by the vulgar realities of life. When the going got tough, Lucy would...well, actually, the going never did get tough for her. Her child was so well-behaved in most episodes of *I Love Lucy* during the 1953–54, 1954–55, and 1955–56 seasons, he scarcely uttered a peep—primarily because he wasn't around.

Clearly, Lucille Ball craved the heavy interest and hype that a new baby created for the show but didn't much care for the diaper changing, the feeding, and the caring for him, at least on the air. It would

have cramped her freewheeling and nutty style, and taken the show in an entirely different family comedy direction. Since *Lucy* was perhaps the most popular show of TV's first fifty years, it looks as if she made the right choice.

On the other hand, the device of using Little Ricky as a regular character during that last season didn't appear to stifle the show's creativity. The kid was incorporated pretty seamlessly—sometimes as central to the story, often as mere appendage—and Lucy looked reasonably comfortable with it. Of course, by this time she was already a mother twice over in real life, so the mothering came naturally.

Years later, Little Ricky actor Keith would recall how warm his relationship with Lucy was on the set. And it showed. When she finally got around to being a regular TV mom, Lucy Ricardo was as sweet, caring, and attentive as they come.

That, in the end, is what differentiated fictitious mother Ricardo from actual mother Ball. She was probably a lot more traditional a mom in real life than she played on TV. Unlike June and Donna, Lucy never gave the impression she would ever do any vacuuming in her heels and pearls—no matter how much it might have pleased her husband.

Classic Mom-ents

🚺 While in Italy to play a part in the film *Bitter Grapes*, Lucy grows terribly homesick for her baby son Little Ricky as his first birthday approaches. So she tries to figure out a way to get back home, even though Ricky barely notices she's gone.

🚺 Showing that her maternal instinct extends even to dairy products, Lucy disguises a huge block of Italian cheese as a baby to avoid paying duty on it on the journey back from Italy. Her handling of the pungent product freaks out the new mother seated beside Lucy on the flight.

🚺 Lucy is left stranded at the dock as she is about to embark on a cruise, literally missing the boat because she had to kiss Little Ricky goodbye one final time.

🚺 When Little Ricky's drum playing gets on the nerves of her neighbors the Mertzes (Vivian Vance and William Frawley), Lucy defends her son to the point that it threatens her relationship with an increasingly irate Fred and Ethel. Lucy simply believes that the boy can do no wrong. The neighbors beg to differ.

🚺 Lucy comes to the rescue when Little Ricky gets a case of stage fright before his first school music recital. She would later volunteer—along with husband Ricky—to play cameo roles in the boy's class play, a decision that naturally resulted in utter disaster.

"Something's happened to my brain. It's all dried up."
—Lucy Ricardo

Harriet Nelson
(Herself)

The Adventures of Ozzie & Harriet
(Oct. 3, 1952 to Sept. 3, 1966), ABC

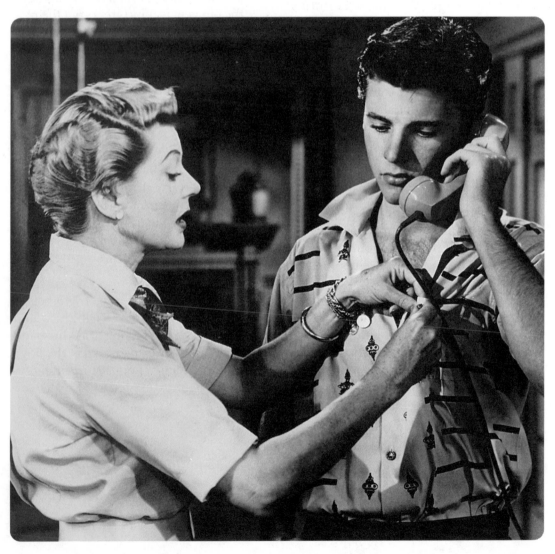

The Adventures of Ozzie & Harriet still holds the record as the longest-running situation comedy in TV history, plowing through fourteen seasons (1952–66) and an astonishing 435 episodes (or more than double the number racked up by *Seinfeld*). Yet despite its massive life span and sheer volume of shows, it can be debated that the program's title was a misnomer. To refer to the storylines as "adventures" requires significant exaggeration.

Indeed, this was one series of adventures that never extended beyond the four walls of the family's home. The man of this uncompromisingly harmonious estate was apparently well-off financially but never appeared to have a job. His wife said "Yes, dear" a lot and then went off to bake pie. The children never encountered any problem more challenging than getting out of helping dad with yard-work or persuading him to let them borrow his car.

But that wasn't even the weirdest thing about *Ozzie & Harriet*. This was: the people starring on the show were an actual family. (Try to imagine Al, Peg, Bud, and Kelly Bundy of *Married . . . With Children* leaving a taping and going home to live together for real.) To get into *Ozzie & Harriet* was to buy into the idea that this is how these people actually behaved with one another, that their trivial dilemmas were genuinely as tough as these lives ever got.

Indeed, many *Ozzie & Harriet* segments appeared to be virtual photocopies of one another. It was all about being upbeat and cheerful. Minutes were spent with the family absorbed in the process of saying hi.

It was "Hi, mom. Hi, pop," followed by "Oh, hello boys. How are you today?" followed by, "Hey, pretty swell. And you?" followed by, "Quite well, thanks for asking."

But if just getting past "How are you?" took up several pages of script, viewers didn't much seem to notice, because dad Ozzie, mom Harriet, and sons Ricky and David were America's family. Why? Because they were on TV. Period. The only time they got interesting at all was when it was discovered that Rick had a talent for music and the show began zealously to promote his career. It was just nice to see *Ozzie & Harriet* get behind something, representing one of the few times that the Nelsons' two lives would intertwine.

While Ozzie played a rather bumbling, easygoing Joe on the series, the truth is that he was apparently a driven tyrant behind the scenes whose insistence that his sons grow up in front of the country left them emotionally scarred for life. At least, this is how those with inside knowledge have described it.

It has also been said that Harriet Nelson's TV demeanor as the wholesome and genteel protector of sons David and Rick was no act. She dispensed warm trays of cookies and cheery words of comfort to the boys both on the set and off. On *Ozzie & Harriet,* however, she was more or less pushed to the background in her prim dress, bopping into the scene to offer up sandwiches and a smile.

No matter. Harriet was the apple pie princess of a doggedly innocent era in TV, even as her family was blurring the lines be-

tween fantasy and reality. The TV Harriet was unique in how little she asked out of life. If her man and two boys were well nourished, she was happy. There has, indeed, never been a less judgmental mom in the annals of telemothering than was Harriet Nelson—whether we're talking the TV version or the genuine article.

Ozzie & Harriet finally went off the air in 1966. Ozzie died in 1975 at age sixty-nine, Harriet in 1994 at eighty-five. And tragically, Rick was killed in a 1985 plane crash at forty-five. A surreal chapter in TV history would perish with them. But Harriet remains with us, because TV moms never really die. They just pass on to cable.

Classic Mom-ents

♀ Harriet Nelson is concerned that her hairstyle is making her look too old and obsesses with her husband Ozzie and sons Rick and David over whether she should change it or not. The prevailing feeling is that Harriet should do whatever makes her feel most comfortable. She keeps her hair as is.

♀ To quell any concerns harbored by the father of the date Rick is taking to a frat party, Harriet suggests to Ozzie that they volunteer as the couple's chaperones. This goes over less than well with Rick and his lady friend, who fear his parents have simply lost their minds.

♀ Harriet is hard-pressed to reassure Ricky when he misinterprets a gesture of friendship from David's girlfriend, tak-

ing it as an expression of romantic interest. He is unsure whether or not he has a responsibility to tell his brother what he suspects. But Harriet assures him that it would open up a can of worms he might not be ready to deal with.

♀ The years are going by, and Harriet is beset by a nagging question: Is teenager David finally old enough to carry his own key for the house? She consults both Ozzie and Ricky on the subject before coming to the conclusion that it might be best to just discuss it with David herself.

♀ Ozzie decides to buy a pool table and convert Ricky and David's old bedroom into a game room after the boys move out. But Harriet won't hear of it, insisting that their room needs to stay the way it is so they will have a comfortable, familiar environment when they come home to visit—which she hoped would be often. Ozzie relents.

"You know, I really hate to admit this, but I can't take all the credit for these pancakes this morning."
—Harriet Nelson

Margaret Anderson
(Jane Wyatt)

Father Knows Best
(Oct. 3, 1954 to Sept. 12, 1960), CBS and NBC

Let it be said at the outset that *Father Knows Best* was blessed with a single novel ideal that wound through its six seasons and 203 episodes. In direct contrast to its family situation comedy competition during TV's first entertainment wave in the 1950s, *FKB* featured a matriarch who had a legitimate clue. The other shows all served up sensible moms and dunderheaded dads, making them essentially, Father Knows Zip.

But the innovations ended right there for a comedy mostly confined by the inane limitations that early television mandated in its shows. The family featured in the program was the Andersons, an unwaveringly wholesome Midwestern clan that never suffered a problem so dire that it could not be solved in twenty-three tidy minutes.

We might presume from the title *Father Knows Best* that it insinuates mother knew least. That, however, was not the case with mommy Margaret (Jane Wyatt), who always appeared to be wearing an apron and carrying something high in saturated fats to feed her hubby Jim (Robert Young) and the kids: seventeen-year-old Betty (Elinor Donahue), fourteen-year-old Bud (Billy Gray), and nine-year-old Kathy (Lauren Chapin).

The thing was, Margaret—while very much a prototypically cheerful cooking and cleaning machine—was also loving and a bit edgy for the times. There were moments during *Father Knows Best* that Marg grew bored with her humdrum daily life, becoming frustrated and demanded some genuine attention herself.

This mom had needs—needs that scraping grime from an oven rack would not fulfill. That ultimately served to differentiate Margaret a bit from her 1950s TV mom contemporaries. There was an individuality hiding underneath that occasionally made itself visible.

But again, most of the time Margaret pretty much went with the program. That meant calmly talking out any problem that cropped up for the kids. When that didn't work, she left it for Jim to deal with after he arrived home from his generic agent's job with General Insurance Company, slipped on a sweater and slippers, and plopped down in his easy chair. From there, dad would launch into his warmth and sensitivity mode to quell any crisis.

You got the feeling that Bud could have rushed into the kitchen screaming, "Mom! Mom! I just shot a man to death with a nickel-plated handgun after our heroin deal went south!" and Margaret would have serenely replied, "OK honey, that may be an issue your father will have an opinion on. Can it wait until he gets home from work?"

Ah, the 1950s. No AIDS, no kids shooting up the schoolyard, no divorce, no single teenage moms. What a time it was to live—at least on TV. No one more successfully navigated that Pleasantville-style utopia than did Margaret Anderson.

Classic Mom-ents

♀ Margaret and her husband Jim are left befuddled when they go off alone together on a weekend retreat. They decide to break the news of this brief vacation gently, and at the last minute. But son Bud and daughters Betty (a.k.a. Princess) and Kathy (better known as Kitten) take the news entirely too well, perplexing their parents. And when Margaret and Jim reach their destination, they call home—and there's no answer! That can only mean one thing: crisis time.

♀ Fed up with her daily housework and child-rearing routine, Margaret busts out of the house and decides to take

some personal time. She goes shopping, eats alone in a restaurant, and creates some drawings while dining. When Jim discovers a drawing Margaret had left behind, he's puzzled and convinced there is more behind this than taking a little break.

⚲ Margaret feels entirely unappreciated by Jim and the kids and rashly decides that she will find a family that doesn't take her dedication to the home and everyone's welfare for granted. She actually plots to disown the Anderson clan outright. But the kids go to great lengths to apologize and reassure Margaret just how much they truly care.

🜛 To help kindle more respect from her husband and kids and make life a little bit more convenient, Margaret decides to learn how to drive. It disturbs her that the kids see her need to get a driver's license as something of a lark rather than a desire for greater responsibility. But she will grow frustrated with the process and abandon her goal in the end.

🜛 For an upcoming PTA costume dance, Margaret hits on the idea that she and Jim should attend wearing the same clothes they had on the day they met. But the outfits are so dorky that the kids express embarrassment that Margaret is their mother. Mom shoots back that she isn't terribly fond of their new fashions, either. So there.

"Sometimes, if a gal is out of options, she needs to use the female art of persuasion to get her way. That's what I do."
— Margaret Anderson

June Cleaver
(Barbara Billingsley)

Leave It to Beaver
(Oct. 4, 1957 to Sept. 12, 1963), CBS and ABC

If there was a per-fect—and perfectly poised—example of telemothering in the early days of series television, it would be June Cleaver, the unflappable, ever-cheery mother to sons Theodore "Beaver" Cleaver (Jerry Mathers) and his brother Wally (Tony Dow) as well as wife to Ward (Hugh Beaumont) on the family sitcom classic *Leave It to Beaver*.

It has been said that June (as ren-dered by Barbara Billingsley) was so singularly flawless in her pearls, her crisp housedress, her apron, her smudge-free makeup, and her shimmering high heels that an entire succeeding genera-

tion of American mothers decided to start careers rather than attempt to be June's equal.

Even while cooking breakfast—which was always a hearty affair of pancakes, eggs, and bacon—June was dressed to the nines, stylishly primped and effortlessly prepared to attack the day by what had to be 7:30 in the morning. Once the kids were off to school and Ward to his accounting office, she would do something even more astounding: vacuum the rugs wearing those high heels! It was a feat worthy of a circus contortionist.

Moreover, June always seemed happy. Every minute of every day. Were an atomic bomb to drop a block away, June would beam that smile, place her manicured hand on Beaver's shoulder and reassure, "Don't you worry, we'll still have our dinner right on schedule."

As this was the time before enlightened attitudes about women serving in the workplace and as equal domestic partners, June stayed home cooking casseroles, worrying, deferring to her husband's judgement, worrying a little bit more, tending the garden, sipping tea, and more or less being exceptionally bland.

Yet there was still something a little bit special about the way Billingsley pulled off being the Martha Stewart of the Cold War era. June displayed a certain charm and earnestness that proved rather infectious, and her laissez-faire child-rearing techniques cleverly mandated personal accountability. June's greatest challenge in life may have been in making sure that youngest son Beaver at least tasted a few of his brussels sprouts, but that was the kind of ersatz, idealized mother image that the times surely demanded.

And so it was. Ward handled the heavy lifting. June covered the domestic chores with her happy mask firmly attached. When the boys screwed up, discipline was eschewed in favor of gentle, homespun humor that usually left Beaver and Wally offering, "Gee, thanks Mom." And Mom would smile and nod her head. And the pearls around her neck would rustle. And everything would be just dandy in Suburban Utopia, USA.

Classic Mom-ents

When friend Eddie Haskell (Ken Osmond) uses his pen to change Beaver's math grade from a D– to a B–, June is not amused. She is initially crushed that her boy would try to mislead her so deliberately. But this is one mother who knows her kid, and June finally guesses correctly that this had Eddie's name written all over it.

Wally has Eddie stay at the Cleaver home for a sleep-over. But things come apart when the two decide to play chess and Beaver catches Eddie cheating. Eddie storms out of the house angry at Beaver and Wally, so June feels compelled to retrieve Eddie to make sure he's inside safely—and that he makes up with Wally.

At school, Beaver is assigned to write an essay about June's life to honor Mother's Day. But when he discovers that her life has been pretty uneventful, he fabricates an extravagant tale about her and hands it in. The teacher suspects fraud and confronts Beaver, also telling his mother. But June is proud of her kid for lending the project such imagination.

For June's birthday, Beaver goes out and buys her the ugliest print blouse anyone has ever seen. But Beaver thinks it's beautiful, of course. June is trapped when Beaver asks her to wear it to the Mother's Club tea the following day. June sacrifices herself rather than risk hurt feelings.

Beaver and Wally get into an intense fight, forcing June to run over and break it up. She tries to explain to the boys how lucky they are to have one another and suggests they write each other notes of apology. Another fight ensues.

"Ward, I'm a little worried about the Beaver."
—June Cleaver

Ruth Martin
(June Lockhart)

Lassie
(Sept. 8, 1958 to Sept. 11, 1964), CBS

While it can be argued that her adopted son Timmy was raised to a significant degree by a wondrous collie named Lassie, Ruth Martin nonetheless performed her motherly duties with dedication and skill.

There are, after all, certain tasks that only a mom can do. And Ruth (June Lockhart) always seemed to have a handle on things, whether it was keeping Timmy (Jon Provost) in clean clothes or making him feel special.

Heck, even Lassie needed someone to put the horse meat and cornmeal in her doggie dish. That daily chore fell to Ruth, who made sure both boy and dog were well-fed and cared for—making her a prairie version of a TV mom who appeared slightly more grounded in reality than did, say, June Cleaver and Harriet Nelson.

Indeed, Ruth was an especially devoted mom considering that Timmy wasn't her natural kid. He was a runaway orphan who had been adopted by the previous inhabitants of the farm where the childless Martins (including husband Paul, played by Hugh Reilly) took over. (Note: Both Ruth and Paul were played for the 1957–58 season by different actors—Ruth by Cloris Leachman, believe it or not, and Paul by Jon Shepodd. Lockhart and Reilly would remain in the roles from 1958–64.)

Ruth, as rendered by Lockhart, was a product of the old school of telemothering. She didn't really serve as a big-time nurturer so much as an older companion who kept Timmy secure and essentially carefree. The real parental heavy lifting, however, fell to Lassie, who would bark enthusiastically whenever the kid did something really dumb that could have gotten him into a fix. Then when the boy found danger anyway, the collie would dutifully save him.

Yet it should be noted that Lassie was in fact something of a fraud. First off, she was a female impersonator. It's true. There were nine collies enlisted to portray Lassie over the years—and all of them were guys (male collies are bigger, boast thicker fur, and never go into heat—which would have wreaked havoc with the production schedule).

There was even a story late in the original Lassie run (the 1970–71 season) when Lassie met a male collie, fell in love, and bore a litter of pups. Quite a trick considering the pooch's true gender.

Ruth certainly suffered no such gender-confusion issues. Lockhart imbued her with a sincere warmth as Timmy's faithful primary caretaker. She was what the era called for in a TV mom: thoughtful, responsible, fairly undemonstrative, and perhaps even a little bit distant. Even so, Ruth gave the kid hugs on a fairly steady basis. That, and a heroic, female-impersonating collie, is all a farm boy could ever really ask for.

Classic Mom-ents

♀ When Ruth entrusts an egg delivery to son Timmy, he and his friend Boomer find themselves harassed by a particularly nasty barn owl while trying to replace two broken shells. It would fall to Lassie to help shoo away the owl. But Ruth winds up distressed nonetheless.

♂ Timmy gets into the habit of delivering "whoppers"—which is the term he uses to describe fabricated stories—to his school chums. This greatly upsets Ruth, who forbids him to lie any longer. But Timmy doesn't want to listen.

♀ Ruth suffers a dilemma when Lassie rebels against the new refrigerator the Martin family has purchased, preferring meals served out of the old one (no cans from the cabinet for this pooch). So Ruth considers getting the old fridge back.

♀ When Ruth finds a half-drowned cat struggling to survive outside their home, Timmy begs her to let the feline (named Marmalade) stay. She agrees.

But when the cat immediately starts getting Lassie into trouble, it's left to Ruth to teach the boy a harsh lesson: that one's heart can be a poor decision-maker, particularly when it comes to adopting pets.

♂ Ruth's worst fears come true when the family members get separated by a thick and dangerous fog while on a camping trip. Timmy is nowhere in sight. Perhaps Lassie could lend a paw in getting out of this mess, no?

"I think it's about time for you and Lassie to come in for supper, Timmy."
—Ruth Martin

Donna Stone
(Donna Reed)

The Donna Reed Show
(Sept. 24, 1958 to Sept. 3, 1966), ABC

If Wonder Bread could somehow take sitcom form, it would look an awful lot like *The Donna Reed Show*, a family comedy that was as divertingly wholesome as it was purposefully mild. And yet, Americans who were around at the time recall the series with the kind of special fondness that has somehow escaped the legacy of such 1950s and 1960s peers as *The Adventures of Ozzie & Harriet* and *Father Knows Best*.

That latter comedy pair have come to represent nostalgic cliches. But while *Donna Reed* was surely cut of the same dullish cloth, it is remembered endearingly—perhaps in part because star Donna Reed was such a queenly and charismatic presence.

Reed's alter ego Donna Stone had a forceful air about her that others of her telemom ilk lacked. She was just plain sturdy. You knew she was in charge of

that suburban castle she shared with her handsome pediatrician husband Dr. Alex Stone (Carl Betz), and kids Mary (Shelly Fabares) and Jeff (Paul Petersen). (The family later added the eight-year-old orphan Trisha—played by Petersen's real-life sister Patty Petersen—to their household.)

Donna was a good and caring mom who took care of her kids' needs, so long as those demands were not weightier than the occasional cookies-and-milk snack after school. That was pretty much as difficult as life got in the lily-white enclave of Hilldale, where not only could you leave your front door unlocked at night, you could leave expensive jewelry sitting on the adjoining sidewalk and it would still be there in the morning. It might even be wrapped up and placed on the porch.

Throughout the

276 episodes of the series, the Stone family's adventures were notably unimaginative and ordinary by today's standards. Mostly, the stories surrounded someone cheating on a test or agonizing over a cat stuck in a tree. Mom never faced an abortion or pondered a lesbian affair. The kids never tried marijuana. They never even dragged on a Chesterfield.

And indeed, Donna was the very essence of flawlessness. The blonde hair was coiffed immaculately. Her dresses were perfectly starched. She kept house like Bill Gates assembles stock portfolios. She always had the right answer to any potential crisis. More often than not, her response to life's knotty little problems was to feed it something sweet and make it go away. Darn if it didn't work every single time.

So while Donna Reed (who died in 1986) likely wished that her greatest legacy had been her work in *It's a Wonderful Life*, it is her namesake TV show that is cited most often. And she has Donna Stone to blame. She was simply too irresistible a TV mom to ignore.

Classic Mom-ents

♀ Jeff Stone comes home from school with a black eye earned in a schoolyard fight. With dad too busy at work to teach his son the "manly arts," it falls to his mother Donna to read a book on fight technique and train Jeff for battle in the backyard. He would learn a bit too well, giving his mother a black eye during training. But Jeff also wins his next fight.

♀ The moral fiber of the Stone family is tested when Jeff finds a winning lottery ticket that could be redeemed for a new Ferrari sports car. But Donna insists that the boy call around and do some legwork to track down the rightful owner—because it's the right thing. Jeff balks. But he ultimately knows that his mother is correct.

♀ Donna grows concerned when a neighbor's window is shattered by a baseball, and Jeff denies any culpability. Slowly, she discredits his alibi and forces the boy to 'fess up. It would be a lesson learned the hard way: one has to tell the truth even when it proves inconvenient. Jeff wouldn't forget it.

♀ When husband Alex and kids Jeff and Mary are involved in three separate events requiring her attendance at the same time, Donna wishes she could clone herself a few times over. She finally figures out a way to frequent each of the three for a short time, only to have a transportation snafu quash her plan.

♀ Donna and hubby Alex have a disagreement over exactly how their first date unfolded. So they each relate the version of events and leave it up to their kids to decide whose memory is more reliable (or unreliable). As it happens, the kids are rather dubious about both accounts.

"Jeffrey, I think it's time you told me the truth, don't you?"
—Donna Stone

Wilma Flintstone (Jean Vander Pyl) and Betty Rubble (Bea Benaderet and Gerry Johnson)

The Flintstones

(Sept. 30, 1960 to Sept. 2, 1966), ABC

In the consistently inspired world of *The Flintstones*, Wilma and Betty came upon their motherhood through decidedly unconventional means. Wilma gave birth to her adorable daughter Pebbles following a pregnancy that appeared to last all of two weeks and swell her tummy from three inches to a mere four and a half inches in diameter. Betty got her boy Bamm-Bamm the old-fashioned way: she picked him up off the doorstep and carried him into the house.

Of course, the fact the show happened to be animated and set in the year 10,000 B.C. may have had a little to do with the strange sense of reality. And it was all in keeping with the off-kilter tenor of a cartoon that was truly ahead of its time in numerous ways.

Until *The Simpsons* arrived a quarter of a century later, *The Flintstones* had been longest-running animated series of all time. It debuted in 1960 as a Friday night program at a juncture when there were no animated shows in primetime. A parody of modern suburban life set in the Stone Age and patterned on *The Honeymooners*, it would endure for six very clever seasons.

The Flintstones led us to believe that before modern civilization sprouted into existence, the world was much like the one of the twentieth century—just much rockier. The story lines centered on a couple of average Joes and Janes living in the tidy prehistoric enclave of Bedrock: Fred Flintstone (voice by Alan Reed) and his wife Wilma (Jean Vander Pyl), and their best friends, Barney Rubble (the great Mel Blanc) and wife Betty (Bea Benaderet, and later Gerry Johnson). The Flintstones also had a pet dinosaur named Dino (also Blanc).

Fred was a loudmouth boob, but a loyal and harmless one. Redheaded Wilma wore the pants in the family and skillfully made

Fred believe he actually did. Barney was even more dense than Fred but was unfailingly moveable, while brunette wife Betty was more quiet but very easy on the eyes.

As mothers, Wilma and Betty were calm, capable, and almost aloof. They tended to let their brain-deprived hubbies do whatever they wanted with the kids, causing some anxious moments. But Pebbles was a cooing cutie, and Bamm-Bamm as well-adjusted as any kid who regularly shook the house while banging a club into the floor could be. Betty never disciplined her son for these regular violent outbursts. The kid was strong enough at the age of one to pick up the house. What could she do?

Besides, Betty and Barney were so happy simply to be parents that light discipline was understandable. They were evidently unable to conceive naturally. So when an orphan was dumped on their doorstep, they were overjoyed. This was yet another area in which *The Flintstones* was groundbreaking: it showed a couple heaping unconditional love and affection onto a child who was not their natural offspring.

Classic Mom-ents

♀ Wilma Flintstone and husband Fred appear to choose beauty over mothering skills when she hires "Annie" to babysit her infant daughter Pebbles. They are unaware that "Annie" is actually the fetching singer and actress Ann-Margrock, and Fred and pal Barney Rubble unknowingly audition for her show.

♀ Betty Rubble wishes upon a falling star for a child and winds up with pint-sized, club-wielding cave tot Bamm-Bamm abandoned on their doorstep. Betty and husband Barney find that their parental instincts kick in when they fight tooth and nail to adopt the orphan kid. They even hire renowned attorney Perry Masonry to plead their case.

♀ While Wilma and Betty are out, babysitters Fred and Barney tote Pebbles to a wrestling match, where she crawls into the ring in the middle of the action. Barney's voice-throwing trick adds a touch of mirth to an otherwise frightful scene. The incident leaves Wilma realizing that parenting is perhaps best left to her.

♀ When Fred yammers on about how easy Wilma's job is, she challenges her husband to switch jobs with her for a day. She works at the gravel pit; he takes care of Pebbles and does the housework. Disaster follows for Fred. Wilma's point—that caring for a baby is no picnic—is well taken.

♀ Betty and Wilma apparently have little fear of turning over their newborns for intense public scrutiny, first entering their children in a Beautiful Baby Contest and later allowing Pebbles and Bamm-Bamm to hit the road as a miraculous singing sensation before they are even old enough to speak. Both moms are immensely proud—and more than a bit freaked out by the whole thing.

"When you act human again, you can golf."
——Wilma

"Which would you rather have: a guilty conscience . . . or dishpan hands?"
——Betty

Laura Petrie
(*Mary Tyler Moore*)

The Dick Van Dyke Show
(Oct. 3, 1961 to Sept. 7, 1966), CBS

Years before Mary Tyler Moore made it (after all) in the big city with her own show, she portrayed one of the 1960s' most conventional—and yet sexy—moms as the feisty and neurotic but ever supportive Laura Petrie, wife of comedy writer Rob (Dick Van Dyke) and mother to all-American kid Ritchie (Larry Mathews).

Dick Van Dyke is remembered as one of TV's true comedy classics, an inspired blend of tight writing and impeccable cast chemistry. Van Dyke and Moore played a happily married—if gloriously dysfunctional—couple, he the breadwinner, she the housewife. The supporting cast featured Morey Amsterdam and Rose Marie as Buddy and Sally, Rob's fellow comedy writers on *The Alan Brady Show* (series creator Carl Reiner portrayed Brady).

41

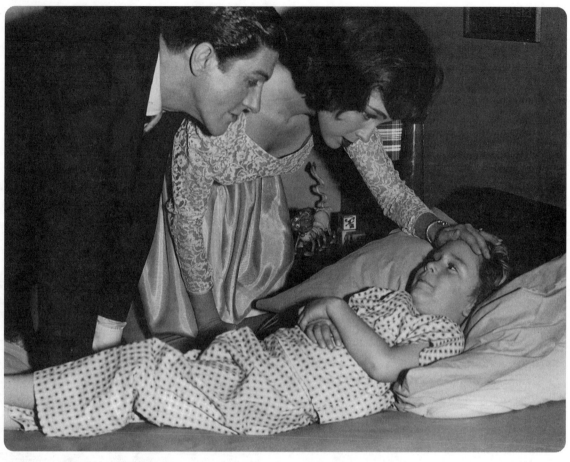

Richard Deacon also had a featured role as show-within-a-show producer Mel Cooley.

Moore's alter ego was always there to lend a dutiful hand and a fine whine while keeping the fires burning in their New Rochelle, New York, homestead. When one thinks of Laura, it is of her swimming in emotional overload and wailing, "Robbbbbbbbb!!!!"

But there was never any question about Laura's rock-solid devotion to her inquisitive Ritchie, who always appeared to be getting sick or saying the wrong thing at the wrong time.

What made Laura especially unique was her ability to rise above the white bread, Ozzie-and-Harriet bent of the early sixties by adding a dash of feminine allure to the mix. While she was a mom to the core, Laura was also a babe, a onetime hoofer (as was Moore in real life) who showed the world that motherhood need not be synonymous with vanilla monotony. Housewives wanted to wear the black stirrup stretch pants that

Moore turned into a fashion fad. Men longed to see what she looked like out of them.

In hindsight, Laura seemed to be the quintessential '90s mom stuck back in the '60s: an intelligent, funny, bold and independent woman who could have pursued that career as a dancer had she not opted instead to stay home and raise the Ritchmeister. She wasn't a full-time mom out of duty but out of choice. That played as downright revolutionary in the age before the feminist movement.

The fact that she was able to remain a terrific mother as well as a fetching spouse helped transform some ingrained notions about TV momhood. Laura was Ritchie's most fervent protector and biggest fan, but we always sensed that she cared at least as much about how she came across both to her husband and to the outside world.

In the role, Moore managed to effortlessly blend warmth and wiles. Laura was nobody's fool, yet she never sacrificed her femininity while making her saucy presence felt in the Petrie home. She could be a nag, sure. But Laura also served to further the evolution of telemothering through her ability to don an apron with such style. Sitcom kitchens have never looked quite the same way since.

Classic Mom-ents

Laura insists that Rob cancel a business trip so he doesn't have to miss six-year-old Ritchie's performance in the school play as a bunny. For Laura, this was serious business: a test of her husband's dedication to home and hearth. Home won out, because this was, after all, the sixties.

Laura skillfully defers to Rob when Ritchie asks the "Where did I come from?" question. Rob handles it with characteristic cluelessness, using it as an opportunity to reflect back on his and Laura's wedding day.

When Laura and her husband throw Ritchie a birthday party, sixty-three screaming kids make a shambles of their home. Laura at first reacts to the bedlam with panic, but when she sees that Rob is freaking out more than anyone, she seizes control of the situation and oversees a mass cleanup.

After one of Ritchie's pair of pet ducks dies, Laura holds the boy's hand and teaches him how to mourn. It is a dark duck day in the Petrie household. But while she is helping her son keep his emotions in check, Laura finds herself more devastated than anyone over the loss—and Ritchie is left to console her.

Ritchie takes to spinning fantastic yarns for some of his school chums, behooving Laura and Rob to instruct him about how lying is bad. However, the situation spins out of control when the parents are called into the school psychologist's office to defend Ritchie's behavior—tapping into Laura's protective instincts.

"Oh Robbbbbbbbb!!"
—Laura Petrie

Jane Jetson (Penny Singleton)

The Jetsons

(Sept. 23, 1962 to Sept. 8, 1963), ABC

The Jetsons was producer Hanna-Barbera's futuristic answer to the Stone Age antics of its well-watched animated half-hour *The Flintstones*. While *The Flintstones* survived and thrived through six seasons in network primetime (1960–66) and stood as the longest-running nighttime cartoon ever until *The Simpsons* came along, *The Jetsons* had just a single season in the primetime spotlight.

And yet *The Jetsons* has proven to be nearly as durable as has *The Flintstones*. After leaving the regular air in 1963, it never really left America's living rooms, rerunning first on Saturday mornings over all three major networks and then later playing in nightly syndication. Then it was revived for the 1984–85 season with forty-one new segments.

Like *The Flintstones, The Jetsons* was creatively wrought with its single-passenger, atomic-powered, flying bubble vehicles, robotic housekeepers, and the use of pneumatic tube technology to dispense children from mid-air to mid-campus.

The Jetson family consisted of dopey dad George (voiced by George O'Hanlon), a futuristic version of a blue-collar worker; George's semi-glamorous, shopaholic wife Jane (Penny Singleton); their typically yappy teenage daughter Judy (Janet Waldo); and tiny cherub son Elroy (Daws Butler). Completing the familial picture were an emotive dog named Astro (voice of Don Messick) and Rosie the Robot Maid (Jean Vander Pyl, who also provided the voice for Wilma on *The Flintstones*).

The Jetsons stories were all engagingly fluffy. And Jane was not only a feisty counterpoint to wimpy George, but also sleek and kind of sexy in a decidedly self-absorbed way. She shopped, she kept house in their modest Skypad Apartments dwelling, she prevented Judy from running off with the teenybopper dweeb of the moment—and she made sure that Elroy didn't destroy himself and others at the controls of some electronic contraption.

But the term that springs most aptly to mind when describing Jane Jetson is classy. She was a classy broad, a telemom of substance, a charming twentieth-century housewife trapped in a twenty-third century family. Jane appeared to be comfortable enough with it; yet she was a TV mother who could have thrived in any era.

Jane gave her kids the independence to become the rambunctious futurists they were destined to be. And when the going got tough, this TV mom got going to the Galaxy Galleria. It was reassuring to observe Jane and note that the retail purchase gene had remained intact even centuries hence. It would prove to be her telemothering legacy.

Classic Mom-ents

🧍 Jane throws her husband George Jetson into a panic when she takes a free one-day trial offer on a robot housekeeper the same night that George is having his boss Mr. Spacely over for dinner—and hitting him up for a raise. When he sees robot Rosie and mistakenly believes his employee must be too rich for the job, Spacely fires George on the spot but later reconsiders in light of Rosie's charming ways. Jane breathes a huge sigh of relief.

🧍 A battle erupts in the Jetson household when Jane insists that she and kids Judy and Elroy need to buy a dog for protection. George objects but finally endorses an apartment-approved electronic dog named Lectronimo. Jane and the kids pick out a real flesh-and-blood dog, and they hold a contest to determine the superior being.

🧍 Fed up with public transportation, Jane decides to take driving lessons to operate her own space vehicle. If son Elroy can get a learner's permit at the age of eight, she figures it should be a snap. But Jane's driving "skills" so agitate her instructor that he quits his job then and there and goes back to hunting wild lions again. Later, Jane's new instructor turns out to be a crook.

🧍 Jane wins a vacation for two on the Love Rocket. But once on board, she runs into her first boyfriend, while George runs into an old girlfriend. Sparks fly anew for both, sending Judy and Elroy scrambling to figure out how to save their parents' marriage before it's too late.

🧍 When Elroy juggles and breaks his mother's favorite pitcher, his first instinct is to cover it up with a lie. But Elroy thinks better of it and admits the truth to Jane, who has a fit. Her son is left wondering: is it better to make up a white lie than to always practice honesty? And will Jane apologize for her overreaction? Elroy ultimately learns that one must (almost) always tell the truth, no matter how much it hurts. And Jane changes her tune to reflect that she's more proud than upset.

"Our home food dispenser broke and I had to wait twenty seconds at the checkout counter. Such ineffilciency!"
—Jane Jetson

Kate Bradley

(Bea Benadaret)

Petticoat Junction

(Sept. 24, 1963 to Sept. 12, 1968), CBS

What can you say about a show that was set in a little railroad town called Hooterville? It would carry an entirely different meaning today, of course. But back in the 1960s, it was all very innocent as the backdrop for *Petticoat Junction*. If it were possible for a show to have been dumber than *Green Acres*, *PJ* was it. And yet it ran for seven seasons and well over two hundred episodes, many of which were cloned from a single concept.

That concept was this: one of the three beautiful daughters of a railroad-town hotel owner gets involved in an ill-advised whirlwind romance. Mom sets them straight. Minutes later, it's as if it never happened.

This turned out to be the premise of at least twenty to twenty-five percent of the *Petticoat Junction* segments. But it didn't matter. This was the sixties, when one didn't necessarily need to be clever to be successful; hence, *PJ* thrived.

It certainly didn't hurt to have a pro like Bea Benadaret presiding over things. She portrayed Kate Bradley, the widowed proprietor of the Shady Rest Hotel, the only public housing facility in all of Hooterville. Kate had the assistance of her trio of fetching young-adult daughters in

46

running things. They were Billie Jo (played by Jeannine Riley, Gunilla Hutton and Meredith MacRae at different times), Bobbie Jo (first Pat Woodell and later Lori Saunders), and Betty Jo (Linda Kaye Henning throughout).

And just to be sure that every white female hair color subgroup was given equal play on *Petticoat Junction,* Billie Jo was blonde, Bobbie Jo a brunette, and Betty Jo a redhead. The girls' portly, bumbling Uncle Joe (Edgar Buchanan)—who was billed as the Shady Rest manager—completed the picture. He had very little hair at all.

The *PJ* stories surrounded trivial crises of one sort or another. One of the girls had fallen for a beatnik, or had located a strand of gray hair on her head which was quickly plucked. Kate wanted to fix one of them up with what was her idea of an eligible bachelor. Once, Kate took a job outside the hotel. Another time, she said "No" to Betty Jo keeping a stray dog.

But what really distinguished Kate as a telemother was her strength and independent spirit in an era when TV moms were overwhelmingly submissive, dependent, and often flighty. Kate was centered and dominant, sometimes to a fault. She could be a control freak in a major way. The girls were all pretty much under moral house arrest at the Shady Rest. It was mom's way or the railway.

Still, no one much seemed to mind that Kate had run the show with an iron fist since her husband Bill died. Somebody had to be in charge, and it wasn't going to be the quasi-bimbettes she had brought into the world. It was one of Kate's great disappointments that she never gave birth to a boy. But she was always there for those girls, serving as both mother and father in the best way she knew how.

Benadaret passed away toward the end of 1968 during the next-to-last season of *PJ.* The show was never the same without her and her great Kate.

Classic Mom-ents

The Shady Rest Hotel is transformed into a giant nursery when daughter Betty Jo's fledgling babysitting business somehow falls into Kate Bradley's lap, forcing her to run it in the interim. Kate is not pleased. Uncle Joe is even less thrilled.

Kate believes she has lost her mind when she finds that one of her guests at the Shady Rest is invisible. And none of her daughters seems inclined to quell any of Kate's fears. But it soon becomes clear that it's one huge practical joke on the part of her girls. Kate, however, would get the last laugh.

Evil landlord Homer Bedloe (Charles Lane) has arranged for the Pixley Bank to foreclose on Kate's mortgage, forcing Uncle Joe and her three daughters (Billy Jo, Betty Jo, and Bobbie Jo) to get jobs. Eviction becomes a real possibility. But then Kate shows her girls a thing or two about defending one's turf by nearly railroading Homer out of town—and keeping the Shady Rest solvent.

♀ Kate seeks advice from Judge Drucker to see if she can legally prevent Billie Jo from running off to Hollywood—believing that she is well within her rights to stop her daughter from doing something that might harm her. But she finds there is no loophole in the law covering youth and stupidity.

♀ When the naive Billie Jo lands a job as the private secretary to a novelist whose books have been banned in Hooterville, the controlling Kate openly questions her wisdom in accepting it. Would this lecherous scribe put moves on her daughter? That was not acceptable. But when Kate has a conversation with the guy, her trust is restored.

"I think family is the most sacred thing in life."
—Kate Bradley

Morticia Addams (Carolyn Jones)

The Addams Family
(Sept. 18, 1964 to Sept. 2, 1966), ABC

Morticia was a glamorous Goth goddess before it was chic, a frightening woman ahead of her time on a TV series that would hit fast and leave faster—though it spawned endless TV versions, spinoffs, and movies in its wake. *The Addams Family* was a magnificently wacky ghoul comedy, and Morticia (played by the late, great Carolyn Jones) proved to be the ghoul with something extra.

Beautiful, sedate, and always dressed in black to match the family mood, Morticia was—underneath all of the dark moods and macabre manifestations—a terrific telemother. She knew just how to make husband Gomez (John Astin), daughter Wednesday (Lisa Loring), and son Pugsley (Ken Weatherwax) feel right at home. Typically, it involved dead flowers and a few blissful hours on the rack. But Morticia understood that was what it took to keep the clan content.

Addams Family would churn out nearly eighty episodes during its scant two-season run, and Morticia's mothering skills were central to nearly every segment. Her versatility was legendary. One minute, she would be snipping the blooms off of roses to piece together an exquisite thorn arrangement; the next, she might be whipping together some antelope blood pudding. It was all in a day's work for this pillar of maternal stability.

Yes, this was a family of freaks, but as outrageous as these people were, they never saw it as anything less than normal to have a disembodied human hand retrieve the mail from inside a black box and keep a pet lion roaming through the house. In hindsight, who would insist that the Addamses were more bizarre than, say, the Simpsons (with their jaundiced skin and strange finger configuration)?

As the crazy glue holding the family together, as it were, Morticia was a scary mom by design. She had nothing to compare it against, having grown up with mutants like Uncle Fester (Jackie Coogan) and the hair-challenged Cousin ITT (Felix Silla). So Morticia thrived in her musty castle of a homestead, even if the outside world seemed to have a difficult time accepting the family's lifestyle.

With the kids, Morticia was protective and ever-doting. With her randy hubby, she was teasing and seductive, taunting Gomez into submission with her slinky moves and French utterances. Frightful though she may have been, Morticia proved to be a perfect TV mom for the mid-1960s—morose, dedicated, level-headed. And deliciously terrifying.

Classic Mom-ents

- Morticia disapproves of the books her children Wednesday and Pugsley are assigned in school, since they portray ghouls, giants, and goblins as the bad guys. So, for the sake of her kids, she sets up shop in a cave and decides to write better stories herself, including, "The Good Giant Slays Sir Lancelot" and "Cinderella, the Teenage Delinquent."

- After the stock market collapses and the Addamses are certain they have lost their nest egg, Morticia rallies the family financially (without telling Gomez) by setting them all up in jobs. She teaches fencing. Fester and Lurch start an escort service. Thing sells pencils.

- Morticia uses reverse psychology on Wednesday to stop her annoying habit of hiding in the house, refusing to search for the girl even when she disappears for hours. Wednesday promptly runs away from home for real, winding up at the police station. Morticia theorizes that her daughter's running away is a good thing, somehow drawing the two closer together.

- Playing mommy to her manservant, Morticia vows that Lurch will finally accept his annual invitation to the Butlers Ball rather than turn it down like he always does. She will teach him to dance! Morticia teaches him to tango, and together they win the night's big trophy.

- When Wednesday is traumatized after being forced to read "Grimm's Fairy Tales" at school, Morticia resolves to keep the children home rather than endure stories in which witches and ogres are killed. She is able to convince the school principal to remove the book from the curriculum.

"Oh Gomez, you just think of me as a plaything."
—Morticia Addams

Lily Munster (*Yvonne DeCarlo*)
The Munsters
(Sept. 24, 1964 to Sept. 1, 1966), CBS

Few think of Lily Munster as a truly progressive TV mom, but frankly it's impossible to come to any other conclusion.

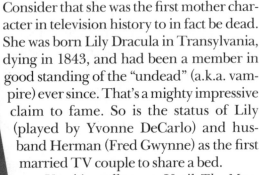

Consider that she was the first mother character in television history to in fact be dead. She was born Lily Dracula in Transylvania, dying in 1843, and had been a member in good standing of the "undead" (a.k.a. vampire) ever since. That's a mighty impressive claim to fame. So is the status of Lily (played by Yvonne DeCarlo) and husband Herman (Fred Gwynne) as the first married TV couple to share a bed.

Yes, it's really true. Until *The Munsters*, married folk on the air were required to sleep in separate twin beds, which had to have made it awfully difficult to conceive the children they always seemed to be popping out. But Lily and Herman snuggled under the same sheets in a queen-size bed, the thinking evidently being that they were kind of like cartoon characters, anyway, so it didn't really count. But it did.

The Munsters was the second of the pair of ghoul-coms to hit the air in the fall of 1964, the other being *The Addams Family*. Whether coincidental or not, the two shows shared virtually identical primetime runs, practically to the day—staying on from September of '64 to September

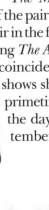

'66. Both were well-received and retain their popularity in reruns today, but they were viewed as gimmicks from the start.

As the matriarch of the eccentric clan who lived at 1313 Mockingbird Lane in Camelot, New Jersey, Lily shuffled around the family's cobweb-covered gothic mansion in her vampiress getup. Husband Herman was your normal, everyday, seven-foot-tall Frankenstein monster lookalike. The couple shared their house of mock horror with crusty vampire Grandpa (Al Lewis), their ten-year-old, werewolf-like son Eddie (Butch Patrick), and their normal-looking niece Marilyn (Beverly Owen and later Pat Priest).

Oh yes. The Munster family also had a dragon named Spot and a black cat named

Tiger as well as a real raven in their cuckoo clock.

Despite their decidedly idiosyncratic appearance and style, the Munsters considered themselves perfectly normal (even if no one else did). That was the joke. To that end, Lily comported herself with utter class and dignity and was always surprised when the family's looks and living situation were seen as anything other than typical.

But Lily was unerringly sweet and easy-going with little Eddie, even if his monsterly instincts would have preferred that his mother let him have it a bit more often. The amusing part was that Lily always consoled Marilyn, whose all-American looks appeared freakish to her fellow family members. To Lily's everlasting credit, she never let her own unease at her niece's conventional beauty get in the way of her love.

Classic Mom-ents

When Eddie's school principal visits the Munster home, he hopes to have a conversation with the boy's parents alerting them to the lad's overactive imagination. But the educator sees for himself that, if anything, Eddie was underplaying his home life. Whatever the reason for the visit, however, Lily is determined to make the principal feel comfortable and help her son's standing in school. She fixes him a lavish snack and arranges for a gracious family reception that doesn't have quite the impact she had hoped for.

Lily is overcome with pride when the Munsters are chosen as the "Average American Family" by Event magazine. She welcomes reporters and photographers assigned to the story into her home and is puzzled by the media's rather unnerved reaction.

A crisis erupts for Lily when she discovers that Eddie is depressed because her fellow family members don't treat him badly enough. Eddie's mother apologizes, promising to ignore and abuse him with greater energy in the future.

When Herman encourages his son Eddie to take on a bully at school, Lily gets involved and tries to put a stop to it. She's fearful that Eddie won't beat the bully badly enough to make it worth his while, a fact that Herman has failed to consider.

In order to show son Eddie and niece Marilyn how much they each still love one another, Lily and Herman vow to buy one another expensive gifts for their one-hundredth wedding anniversary. They both take jobs as ship welders to earn the extra money, not realizing the other is there. Madcap mix-ups ensue.

"Grandpa, you stop being a bat this instant!"
—Lily Munster

54

Samantha Stephens (Elizabeth Montgomery) and *Endora* (Agnes Moorehead)

Bewitched

(Sept. 17, 1964 to July 1, 1972), ABC

Not only was Samantha Stephens the prettiest witch in network television history, she was also one of the most charming, devoted, and energetic TV moms ever. But it turned out that *Bewitched* would be blessed with not one but two memorable mamas. The show also gave the world Endora, Sam's moody, haughty witch of a mom. To-

gether, the two of them added up to pure motherly magic.

Bewitched was actually the vehicle handpicked by the show's producer-director, William Asher, to star Elizabeth Montgomery (Samantha). Usually, it's the other way around: You have a concept first and then cast it later on. But it was different this time for one key reason: Asher happened to be married to Montgomery in real life.

The show that Asher crafted for his wife turned out to be a smash hit that would crack the Nielsen ratings Top 10 each of its first three years on the air (1964–67) and then finish eleventh in the two subsequent seasons. It starred Montgomery as Sam, a nose-twitching witch who married a very mortal and neurotic ad executive named Darrin (Dick York and later Dick Sargent).

That Samantha would marry out of her faith, as it were, continually infuriated her self-righteous and somewhat vindictive mother (the terrific Agnes Moorehead). To gain a measure of revenge, mom Endora habitually cast embarrassing spells on Darrin, once turning him insufferably self-centered and another time causing him to slowly shrink. For Darrin, it was like having Satan for a mother-in-law. But for Endora, it proved to be wonderful sport.

Samantha often had little success in keeping her willful mom from transforming her husband into inanimate objects. But Sam had somewhat better control over her little girl Tabitha (played primarily by identical twins Erin and Diane Murphy), who arrived in Sam and Darrin's life during the January 13, 1966 broadcast. A son, Adam (portrayed by twins David and Greg Lawrence), came along on October 16, 1969 but didn't appear regularly until 1971.

For the most part, Sam's mothering centered on the mischievous Tabitha. And her job as a mother typically involved reversing Tab's early stabs at casting spells and hiding the evidence. Considering Endora's maturity level, Tabitha pretty much represented Samantha's second child.

Yet as frazzled as she had to feel simply trying to keep her husband from getting banished to another dimension and her mother and daughter from exposing their witchy powers to Darrin's boss or their nosy neighbors, Sam was quite a lovely lady and very much a tender and caring mother. She single-handedly gave witches, and witches with half-witch and half-mortal offspring, a good name forever.

Classic Mom-ents

⚲ Tabitha uses her powers of witchcraft to turn a boy playmate into a bulldog and doesn't know how to change him back. Samantha, desperate to control the damage, stalks the dog as he digs up a neighbor's flower bed and twitches up a badge that designates her a dog catcher. It works.

⚲ Endora has an emergency appointment at the Taj Mahal and quickly brings a toy soldier to life to babysit Tabitha. But after Endora leaves, Tab mimics all of her grandmother's gestures to bring all of the toys in her room to life.

♀ Samantha is helpless in trying to hide a polka-dotted toy elephant that Tabitha has twitched to life while Darrin's boss Larry Tate (David White) and a home appraiser are at the Stephens home. But Sam is somehow able to convince the men that Darrin bagged the elephant—polka dots and all—while on safari in Africa.

♂ Impatient with Darrin's slow progress in learning Italian to help him land an important account, Endora decides to speed things up by casting a spell that makes him speak like a native. Darrin's limited English is left thickly accented, however, leaving his boss to think he is mocking the Italian account executives.

♂ When Larry Tate sees a fully-grown pony rising out of Tabitha's crib, he assumes the Stephens house is haunted. It is only Tabitha using her developing witchy powers without permission. But Samantha, as usual, is able to save the day, making Tate believe he has simply had too much to drink.

"Mother, Darrin's gone and somebody's got him!"
—Samantha

"Who'd want him?"
—Endora

1928 *Porter*
(Ann Sothern)

My Mother the Car
(Sept. 14, 1965 to Sept. 6, 1966), NBC

One of the most bizarre and undeniably beloved comedies to emerge from the escapist bent of the 1960s was this camp classic about a small-town lawyer (Jerry Van Dyke) whose mother (voiced by Ann Sothern) dies and is reincarnated as an automobile—specifically a 1928 Porter. (There was actually no such car as a Porter. The auto used in the show was a renovated Ford. The name Porter was taken from a production assistant.)

The idea of an old woman returning to life as a piece of machinery was very much

son Dave Crabtree (Van Dyke) found mom when he purchased her second-hand at an antique car lot, a rusted heap of junk that he renovated. Mom spoke to him through the car radio, which lit up and flickered with each syllable. Their banter was never biting, always thoughtful.

Dave was the only one whom mom would talk to in her new "body." To her son, she was warm, witty, and only occasionally cynical. Dave's wife, Barbara (Maggie Pierce), was likewise thrilled to have the Porter around, if for no other reason than it seemed to keep her husband so happy. She remained blissfully ignorant of the mother aspect—as was everyone else.

Except for the fact one of them was powered by an internal combustion engine, the interaction between mom and son was uncannily typical. They essentially looked out for one another whenever trouble lurked, which was basically anytime an antique car collector named Captain Manzini (Avery Schreiber) was nearby. Manzini was constantly plotting to get the Porter away from Dave. But having just the one season with which to operate, he simply ran out of time.

While the show was clearly a high-concept novelty, *My Mother the Car* ironi-

in sync with an era that gave us shows centered around a shapely genie (*I Dream of Jeannie*), a beautiful witch (*Bewitched*), a group of zany castaways (*Gilligan's Island*), a family of contemporary ghouls (*The Addams Family*), a clan of bumbling, loveable Nazis (*Hogan's Heroes*) and—somewhat unfathomably—a flying nun (*The Flying Nun*).

My Mother the Car would last for just a single season. But it nonetheless stood out as a surprisingly sweet and gentle show. Her

cally featured one of the more engagingly loyal relationships between a mother and a grown son as has ever graced primetime.

Words to the *My Mother the Car* opening theme:

Everybody knows in the second life we
  all come back sooner or later;
As anything from a pussycat to a man-
  eating alligator;
Well you might just think my story is
  more fiction than it's fact;
But believe it or not my mother dear
  decided she'd come back...
As a car.
She's my very own driving star.
A 1928 Porter;
That's my mother dear;
She helps me through everything I do;
And I'm so glad she's here *(two beeps
  on horn).*
My mother the car... My mother the
  car."

Classic Mom-ents

♂ When Dave, his wife Barbara, and their two kids take his mom to a drive-in to satisfy her urge to watch the Sonny Tufts Film Festival, an escaped convict menaces the family and commandeers the mom/car at gunpoint. Mom spins the car in circles until the dizzy crook drops his gun and collapses.

♀ Barbara is talking to the car in the family kitchen and asks her why Dave always raved about her buttermilk pancakes. Mom's reply: "That's easy. There's no buttermilk in 'em." She later believes she dreamed the entire incident.

♀ After a female reporter catches wind of the fact that a mother is inside an automobile, the journalist begins talking to mom deliberately, somehow presuming senility. "Can...you...talk?" she asks. Mom replies, "Yes...No...com...ment."

*"Please take me for a spin,
David."
—My Mother The Car*

Joan Nash (*Patricia Crowley*)

Please Don't Eat the Daisies

(Sept. 14, 1965 to Sept. 3, 1967), NBC

The short but significant life of television's *Please Don't Eat the Daisies*—not to be confused with the best-selling book (by author Joan Kerr) or the 1960 Doris Day film of the same name—is noteworthy for its contribution to the legacy of telemothering. Simply put, Joan Nash was a revolutionary, a moldbreaker, an original. The reason: she was genuine.

Back in the mid-1960s, TV was still recovering from the absurd idealism and innocence pioneered by the Donna Stones, the Margaret Andersons, the June Cleavers, and the Harriet Nelsons. Moms of the tube were still programmed to be tireless and cheery cleaning machines who dispensed nurturing and homespun wisdom with all the conviction and believability of a Pez dispenser.

Then came Joan (snappy work from Patricia Crowley). She was a newspaper columnist married to a college English professor named Jim (Mark Miller) who lived in suburban Ridgemont,

New York, with their four kids: Kyle (Kim Taylor), Joel (Brian Nash), and seven-year-old twins Tracey (Joe Fithian) and Trevor (Jeff Fithian).

Not all that terribly weird so far. But here was the kicker: Joan hated housework! And mind-boggling and blasphemous though it may have seemed then, she hated to cook too! Moreover, she didn't give two hoots what any of the gossipy housewives in her neighborhood thought about her peculiar ideas of being a wife and mother.

Having a TV mom in 1965 who couldn't stand the usual wifely domestic chores was more than just atypical. It was akin to being a Communist, or some variety of space alien. And yet Joan still managed to be a smart, relatively together, and devoted mother in spite of foibles as rising at noon and doing whatever she felt like doing that day.

When she wasn't using her life as fodder for her newspaper columns, Joan immersed herself in the usual mayhem that accompanied being the mother to four rambunctious pre-adolescent boys. They all accepted Joan's eccentricities with grace and humor, and often more effectively than did her more stuffy hubby. The family's 150-pound sheepdog, Ladadog, also didn't seem to mind Joan's approach to life so long as there was a doggie treat to be scrounged.

Alas, *Please Don't Eat the Daisies* survived just two seasons. But its offbeat legacy lives on in the quirky Joan—an untraditional gem.

Classic Mom-ents

♂ Joan gives her two oldest sons, Kyle and Joel, the responsibility of taking care of twins Tracey and Trevor. The boys go about their duty by demanding military precision of the twins to prove which of them is more responsible. Mommy Joan winds up believing she is raising two boys for the White House and two for the Foreign Legion.

♂ When the boys demand a fat percentage of the money Joan received for writing an article about their antics, she starts to fear she is raising a brood of greedy little capitalists. Is Joan herself to blame? She starts to think so.

♂ It's a day in domestic hell for Joan when the boys somehow lock themselves inside a bathroom, and Joan gets her hand stuck inside the kitchen garbage disposal while trying to retrieve a ring. She wonders why crises seems to follow her and her kids everywhere they go.

♀ A frantic Joan rushes off to an auction featuring her son's artwork after accidentally fastening one of her and husband Jim's tax returns to the back of the project. Her very standing in the community is suddenly at risk, not to mention her motherly pride.

♀ Joel and Kyle try out for the school play. But Joan believes—and her husband agrees—that neither boy has much in the way of acting talent. Joel is denied a part in the production and takes to sulking, leaving it to Joan to repair her son's wounded pride.

"No, no, I'm serious. You can't buy that painting. It has my tax return glued to the back."
—Joan Nash

Julia Baker
(Diahann Carroll)

Julia
(Sept. 17, 1968 to May 25, 1971), NBC

Julia represented a milestone not only for telemotherhood but for sitcom integration as well, giving a boost to the upscale African-American role model. That was an oxymoron in 1968 before Diahann Carroll was cast in this comedy series as Julia Baker, a young, black, widowed single mother who lands a job as a nurse in the show's first episode.

Now this was big stuff back then. How big? Carroll was the very first black actress to be cast as the lead in a TV comedy. Her role of Julia represented the first female black character in a situation comedy to be depicted in a relatively prestigious way, meaning she wasn't cast as a maid or a poor sharecropper or a welfare recipient.

It was a significant step forward in TV's racial evolution. Carroll's only true female African-American predecessor in terms of a breakthrough role was that of Nichelle Nichols, who portrayed Lieutenant Uhura on TV's original *Star Trek* from 1966 to 1969.

That *Julia* survived for three seasons completed the triumph of a show that boasted a completely integrated cast. Julia's

65

Julia was a nurse, which meant weird hours and exhausting shifts. It also forced her kid to be quite independent and secure (what with his mother working many nights). Luckily, Corey was that. He took after his mom, a proud, saucy, individualistic and self-assured sort who depended on neither the government nor the kindness of strangers.

With Corey, Julia enjoyed a super-tight bond that was fully cemented after the man in their lives was tragically snatched away by death. But neither of them whined. They simply carved out a life together. If Julia had an occasional tendency toward aloofness, the kid was adept at snapping mom out of it.

best friend in the series was black, but the closest pal of her six-year-old son Corey (Marc Copage) was a white neighbor. The mother and son lived together in a racially mixed apartment building in Los Angeles following the death of her husband, and Corey's father, while serving in Vietnam.

So she was a smart TV mom, this Julia. And as Carroll sensed that her character was being counted on as something of a test case, the actress was sure to keep Julia centered and doggedly moral. There was likewise a strident edge to her, but that's probably true of any vigilant mom. And Corey never seemed to complain.

Classic Mom-ents

♀ Julia's six-year-old son Corey tries to tell his mom that he has homework in his second-grade class, which should excuse him from doing his chores around the house. But Julia lets it be known that being lazy and black will get him nowhere in life, and the time to guard against that is now.

♀ A famous professional football player puts fancy moves on Julia, and it's clear the guy usually gets the woman he wants. But Julia is unimpressed by the man's self-centeredness and over-confidence, and gives him the not-so-subtle cold shoulder after Corey shares his dislike for the guy. It was to be Julia's rule: if Corey couldn't warm up to a man, neither could his mother.

♀ When Corey runs for president of his elementary school, he gets a bit caught up in the fervor of the campaign and makes promises he can't possibly keep—leaving it to Julia to guide him back down to earth even as she nurtures his feisty spirit and ambition.

♀ Julia's fellow nurse friend Hannah Yarby (Lurene Tuttle) encourages the widowed Julia to sign up with a computer dating service. But Julia finds her enthusiasm half-hearted, having reserved any energy she doesn't exert at work for her time at home with Corey.

"You know, you may be number one, but I have to tell you that one just happens to be the lowest number you can be—— except for zero."
—Julia Baker

~2~
The 1970s
Dishes and Denial

As the 1970s dawned, things looked pretty much as they did in the '60s. There was the new Mrs. Brady (Florence Henderson), having taken her three very lovely girls and moved in with her new hubby and those three boys of his own. If *The Brady Bunch* seemed at the outset like a forward-thinking look at a blended family, that possibility quickly faded. For one thing, these were not divorced people joining forces, but widowed parents. That kind of took controversy out of the mix.

Yet as played by Henderson, there was a luminous quality to Carol Brady as a mom to three and stepmom to three more. She never played favorites, never waned in her enthusiasm for the job of housewife, never went off on a single drunken binge, never felt trapped, and always had the perfect answer while mediating the trivial feuds of her clean-scrubbed, pasty-white brood. Her greatest challenge came in policing bathrooms in the morning—and even this, Carol accomplished with a winning smile loaded with gleaming white teeth.

Shirley Partridge (Shirley Jones) was the matriarch behind what was perhaps an even more mythical, surrealistic creation on *The Partridge Family*. A widow with five kids, her message surrounded something like, "The family that plays together, stays together." She was a woman in her forties, singing in a pop-rock band astride a genuine teen idol (real-life stepson David Cassidy) and the world's most annoying adolescent (future

ex-con Danny Bonaduce). She was as loving as she was in denial, her success in this world akin to Martha Stewart making it while playing lead guitar for Metallica. At least she wasn't another selfless motherly waif.

Still, just when it began to seem as if the TV mom was destined to forever be cast as terminally uncool, out of nowhere popped some colorful personalities to inject a whole lot of fresh life into the picture.

If the 1970s was the decade when such majestically featherweight TV mom caricatures as Carol and Shirley and retro-icons like Marion Cunningham *(Happy Days)* held court, it was also the era when telemothering began to mature thanks to a producer named Norman Lear. A few moms on the tube grew some warts to go along with the usual freckles, including Edith Bunker *(All in the Family)*, Maude Findlay *(Maude)*, Florida Evans *(Good Times)*, and Louise Jefferson *(The Jeffersons)*. And Lear gave birth to all four of them.

It is difficult to overstate Lear's impact on the TV entertainment landscape. His shows single-handedly transformed prime-time television and the perception of TV motherhood with it. While other producers were caving in to the networks and their narrow, sanitized view of the American family, Lear boldly pushed the envelope to showcase character flaws, foibles, and failings—celebrating their humanity all the while.

In the process of revolutionizing the TV comedy universe, creator-producer Lear presented us with the aforementioned quartet of classic telemoms who embodied a diverse new cross-section of the motherly art. His first unparalleled TV mom creation must have seemed on the surface to have been a giant step backward: Edith (Jean Stapleton), the dimwitted but guileless wife of racist, sexist pig Archie (Carroll O'Connor) on *All in the Family*.

Maude would spin off from *All in the Family* in 1972 and become Lear's second straight hit thanks to the sassy work of Bea Arthur as the ever-opinionated Maude Findlay. Whereas Edith was introverted and docile, Maude was blustery and domineering, a wildly successful counterpoint to the submissive, mannered suburban creature who had come to represent American motherhood in the 1950s and '60s.

But Lear wasn't finished with us just yet. He next spun a show for Maude's maid Florida (Esther Rolle) called *Good Times*. It made its first appearance in February 1974, giving America its first sitcom taste of life inside a lower-middle-class black family (a.k.a. "the 'hood") and a mother who evoked a homespun wisdom that helped her to rise high above her circumstances. In Florida, TV audiences were introduced to a ma who had it tougher than any other yet neither lost her sense of humor nor her focus.

And then there was Louise Jefferson (Isabel Sanford) of Lear's *Jeffersons*, a mom who was able to "move on up" without allowing her head to grow on out. She came to represent the flip side of Florida: materially wealthy and yet not pompous or overbearing. Through Louise, Lear was able to explore another largely untapped area of the maternal psyche that brought a genuine class-consciousness to the table.

Aside from Lear's mothers, the '70s also introduced Ann Romano (Bonnie Franklin), who on *One Day at a Time* showed us that it was possible to divorce, raise two teenage daughters essentially by oneself, and come out all right—even when those daughters proved to be a handful. Plenty of angst likewise coursed through the veins of mom Kate Lawrence (played by Sada Thompson) on the ABC nighttime soap *Family*. Her kids did stuff like marry people who were terminally ill.

Yet the decade wasn't merely about angst and challenges. The most burdensome choice ever faced by Marion Cunningham (Marion Ross) on *Happy Days* was whether or not to treat her frisky husband (Tom Bosley) to a little romp in the marital sack. And no one will ever mistake Robin Williams' sudden bout with motherhood as alien Mork on *Mork & Mindy* as an especially traumatic event. Then again, some might view giving birth to a full-grown Jonathan Winters as an emotional ordeal in its own right.

There were likewise plenty of TV shows during the era that stuck even closer to the ubiquitous three "D's" of telemothering (doting, detachment, and denial), including *The Waltons* and its blissfully fertile matriarch Olivia Walton (Michael Learned) and *Eight is Enough,* with its tirelessly upbeat stepmom Abby Bradford (Betty Buckley).

Yet for all of its Bradys and Partridges and Bradfords, the 1970s managed to be a period of real expansion in the growth and development of the TV mom. And things were about to change even more significantly as tube mothers ventured out of the kitchen and into the workplace.

Carol Brady *(Florence Henderson)*
The Brady Bunch
(Sept. 26, 1969 to Aug. 30, 1974), ABC

She represented the last gasp of no-muss, no-fuss mothering on TV, showing us it was possible to blend two families and six children of both genders and pull it off as easily as one might purchase a bag of groceries. Life was surely a cabaret for a dedicated optimist named Carol Brady (the effervescent Florence Henderson), who would eventually be seen as the ultimate 1970s mom via *The Brady Bunch.*

The show ran from 1969 through '74, growing to become part of the pop culture landscape in the process. Because it bridged the eras of both sitcom innocence and enlightenment (which can be pegged primarily to the premiere of *All in the Family*), *The Brady Bunch* would be viewed through a kitsch-y filter all the way through its uncommonly wholesome five-season run.

If you know the theme song, you know the story: widow with three blonde-haired daughters marries widower with three sons who are roughly the same age as the girls. They instantly form a six-kid

household, with a wiggy housekeeper named Alice (Ann B. Davis) and a shaggy dog named Tiger also included in the mix. So anyhow, this lady links up

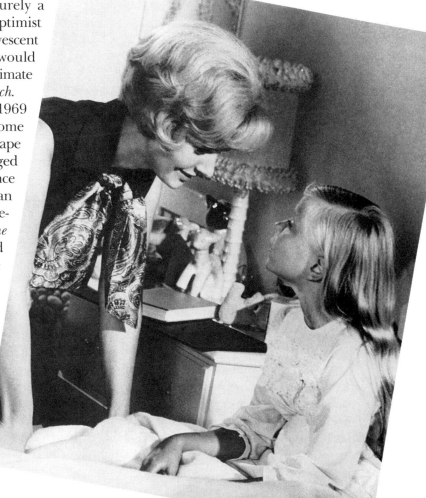

simplistic brew was a new bride and new stepmom by the name of Carol Brady.

Carol's view of life was so bright and shiny that it made the sun itself seem a bit dim by comparison. And why not? Her children (even the ones who technically weren't hers) positively glowed with Caucasian vigor, her marriage proved to be instantly rock-solid beyond measure, and her most challenging issue was whether or not to frost her hair. She sang, she worshiped, she went to PTA meetings, she did needle-point and pottery, and she looked really sexy in cowboy outfits.

To be Carol Brady was to be truly blessed. She and the expanded family lived a serene middle-class existence in a perfect, four-bedroom, two-bath house in the suburbs of Los Angeles. And Carol was entirely comfy with dispensing sage advice to the kids while plugged into the insignificant travails they all faced daily. *The*

with this fellow, Mike Brady (played by Robert Reed). And as it happens, their lily-white brood takes to this overwhelming new situation like toddlers to ice cream. And the straw that was primarily responsible for stirring this

74

Brady Bunch stories rotated between puppy love, vacation snafus, bathroom hogging, tonsillitis, and scouting misadventures.

Somehow, the original series spawned a couple of theatrical films and a pair of short-lived follow-up TV series starring many members of the original cast. And Henderson has grown comfortable with the idea that this Carol Brady thing is probably going to follow her forever, so she might as well enjoy it and make a few bucks in the process.

Carol is having the last laugh. And that's all a telemothering icon could ask for.

Classic Mom-ents

To show the kids that gender roles need not be ingrained and stereotyped, Carol and husband Mike decide to switch places—with Carol teaching the boys to play baseball and Mike helping the girls with a cooking lesson. It is never considered, however, to have Carol instruct the boys in cooking and Mike teach the girls baseball.

A disaster begins to unfold when Carol loses her voice prior to singing "O Come All Ye Faithful" at the annual Christmas morning services. However, youngest daughter Cindy (Susan Olsen) cuts a deal with Santa Claus to bring Carol's voice back just in the St. Nick of time.

When Carol is forced to leave town to help an ailing aunt, everything falls apart in the Brady household. Housekeeper Alice somehow sprains her ankle playing Chinese checkers, re-

quiring Mike to pinch-hit and do all of the chores. The chaos is frightful, but all is right again in Bradyville when Carol returns.

Carol lets Mike talk her into going out and allowing older kids Greg (Barry Williams) and Marcia (Maureen McCormick) to babysit their four younger siblings. Neither of the adults is able to have a good time and are so sick with worry that they return home early. They nearly get arrested for driving so fast on the way—a very un-Brady thing to do.

While getting used to new glasses, middle daughter Jan (Eve Plumb) accidentally crashes her bicycle through a portrait of the kids that Mike had commissioned as a gift for Carol. Hoping to replace the picture with no one the wiser, Jan has another one taken. But her glasses (which didn't appear in the first picture) give the whole scam away. Instead of being upset, Carol is merely touched that her kids, especially Jan, would go to so much trouble to try to make it right.

"Money and fame are very important things. But sometimes there are things that are more important——like people."
——Carol Brady

Shirley Partridge (*Shirley Jones*)
The Partridge Family
(Sept. 25, 1970 to Aug. 31, 1974), ABC

Could you maybe see Madonna's mother going out on tour with her, sharing the stage, carrying backup vocals and handling the keyboards? How about the Red Hot Chili Peppers? Do you think any of their members would toss their kids up on stage to play a few numbers, then go back and record with them on an album? No?

Well then, you now have some idea of how it seems in hindsight that a pop music group—even a fictitious one created for a TV show, as was the case with *The Partridge Family*—would have mom front and center as they crooned, "I think I love you." This was life for one Shirley Partridge (Oscar-winning musical actress Shirley Jones) between 1970 and '74. And miraculously, no one laughed at any of this. The show was, in fact, a smash for a few years. The great thing about Shirley Partridge is that whether or not you believed the admittedly farfetched concept, she was a mother who emerged as strong, centered, and lively, not to mention highly independent. That represented a vast departure from the submissive, superficially jubilant moms like Carol Brady who up until that time had predominated.

Here we had a woman who was a recent widow with five kids living quietly in a Northern California suburb when she stumbled into recording a hit single. Before you knew it, she had packed up her two

teenagers (real-life stepson David Cassidy and the waif-like Susan Dey), her freckled, wisecracking ten-year-old (the notorious Danny Bonaduce), and her pair of tiny tots, put them on a bus to travel the country, and presto, a band was born.

All of the kids played onstage, or at least stood around and looked busy. And Shirley ran the show with surprising ease. This woman had her act together—and then literally took another one out on the road. And as if handling spoiled musicians weren't challenging enough, she also had

to keep a close eye on her group's child-intolerant, directionless manager Reuben Kinkaid (David Madden).

Not all of Shirley's touches fit together so smoothly. No one ever could figure out what the story was with that bus, which resembled something out of an acid trip. All of their songs wound up kind of sounding the same, too. But to be fair, that stuff really is outside of a mother's control. It was an impressive feat just to get everyone to the gig, dressed and bathed properly and without need to take a potty break in mid-show.

The truth is that while Cassidy became a teenybop idol through his lead vocals and dreamboat looks, and The Partridge Family crossed over to become a huge success on the pop charts as well as on TV, it wouldn't last long. That may have been due in part to the fact that none of these people were real musicians. They used studio pros on their albums. But no one seemed the wiser—or to care.

All that really mattered was that Shirley Partridge was a real mom, warm and wholesome and reassuring. At the end of the day, that proved to be the sweetest music of all.

Classic Mom-ents

👫 The recently widowed Shirley Partridge joins her kids' rock band following an impromptu recording session in the garage. She buys a used school bus, paints it psychedelic colors, dresses herself and her brood in matching maroon velvet costumes, and promptly books their first gig in Las Vegas—where the kids are all felled by stage fright.

👫 When Danny accuses the family of being a bunch of big fat lie tellers, Shirley challenges everyone to see if they can practice total honesty for one full day. It would prove to be tougher than anticipated.

👫 Shirley quits the band when a self-serving promoter suggests that it would be in everyone's best interests were she to drop out before a Partridge Family Tour of Europe. But the kids all conspire to make her reconsider.

👫 After Shirley is voted "Mother of the Year" by a women's magazine, she and the kids are invited to attend a banquet in her honor in Sacramento. Shirley decided to drive the family in their tour bus but neglects to take along any money, is slapped with a speeding ticket, and finally runs out of gas in the middle of nowhere.

👫 Shirley punishes her younger children Chris (Brian Forster) and Tracy (Suzanne Crough) when they refuse to clean up a mess they made. They respond by running away from home, winding up at Reuben Kinkaid's house.

"And you, young lady . . . if you had cleaned your own toy box, your Squeaky Weeky wouldn't be missing!"
—Shirley Partridge

Edith Bunker
(Jean Stapleton)

All in the Family
(Jan. 12, 1971 to Feb. 24, 1980), CBS

It would be easy to dismiss Edith Bunker as a dull-witted second banana to her blustery, bigoted, stereotype-spewing stooge of a husband, Archie (Carroll O'Connor). But it would also be wrong, for in Edith actress Jean Stapleton crafted a deceptively kind and righteous woman who gave the brilliant *All in the Family* its very soul.

Her husband referred to her as "Dingbat" in a not-so-loving way, and it was clear that Edith was hardly a scholar. Still, she made up in uncompromising honesty and goodness what she lacked in smarts, and that extended to her sweetly supportive and protective relationship with grown daughter Gloria (Sally Struthers) and son-in-law Mike Stivic (Rob Reiner). She was devoid of prejudice, making Edith the antithesis of the hateful (if curiously principled) Archie. Edith was her bigoted husband's conscience; that made her America's sweetheart as well.

In her own nasal-ly way, Edith was as strong as TV moms come, standing up fearlessly to anyone and anything that made Gloria uncomfortable. It was one of the consistent trademarks that helped make *All in the Family* the distinctive comedy classic it remained from the night it went on the air through its last hurrah.

In fact, it's rather impossible to oversell the impact *All in the Family* had on the primetime network TV landscape. The show literally ruled the tube from 1971 to '76, finishing first in the Nielsen ratings for an unprecedented five consecutive seasons. And the Norman Lear-created comedy changed the course of TV by busting down previously locked creative doors, with its jarringly edgy characters and controversial subject matter.

Edith brought as much comic flair and dramatic tension as anyone, often serving

as an uncomprehending foil. But dingbat or no, Edith also had a mind of her own. She questioned her faith in God when a friend—a female impersonator, no less—was murdered. She confronted a waitress who hit on her husband. She lost her job at a convalescent home for helping honor an invalid woman's wish to die with dignity. Edith also, famously, fought off a rapist at gunpoint in her own living room.

So it's clear that Edith Bunker was nobody's fool. Let's face it, any woman who could stand to live with the incessant rants and raves of Archie deserves an honor of some sort. Edith never got that, but she did receive the wholehearted love and devotion of an adoring daughter who always called her Ma. Their bond carried a special affection, in large measure because Edith loved her unconditionally.

Classic Mom-ents

♀ Edith agrees to join daughter Gloria in protesting the latest Bunker family brawl, storming out of the house and spending the night on their own in a hotel to get the point across that verbal abuse cannot be tolerated. It is unclear whether mother or daughter has inspired the rare show of defiance, but it doesn't really matter.

♀ After Gloria is the victim of an attempted sexual assault, Edith holds her hand and tries to provide guidance as her daughter endures the traumatic legal aftermath of reporting the crime.

♀ Edith is chosen to appear in a TV commercial but finds herself unable to lie when she begins to have qualms about the quality of the sponsor's laundry detergent. Daughter Gloria is proud to see her unfailingly honest mom putting her principals over profits.

♀ When Gloria and her husband Mike decide to skip a special farewell dinner she'd planned in their honor to mark their move to California, Edith is devastated. But she ultimately decides to deal with her anger rationally rather than spinning out of control and attacking.

♀ Edith's cousin Floyd abandons his nine-year-old daughter Stephanie (Danielle Brisebois) on the Bunker doorstep, and immediately Edith insists that the girl move in permanently—her well-honed motherly instincts kicking into overdrive.

♀ Edith turns out to be the sole mourner at her Aunt Rose's funeral, but her resolve to honor the woman is undiminished. The example she sets in doing what she believes to be the right thing touches daughter Gloria in an almost magical way, making her proud to be Edith's little girl.

"I don't know if that's such a good idea, Archie."
—Edith Bunker

Maude Findlay
(Beatrice Arthur)

Maude
(Sept. 12, 1972 to April 19, 1978), CBS

As the first spinoff from *All in the Family* by legendary creator-producer Norman Lear, *Maude* would enjoy a successful six-season run throughout the middle of the 1970s.

In the blustery, saucy, outspoken, upper-crust, ultra-liberal Maude Findlay (originally cast as Edith Bunker's cousin on that other show), TV audiences were treated to a female left-wing version of Archie Bunker. Both were equally loud and obnoxious—and somehow lovable, anyway. Maude was to TV mothers what forest fires are to nature. She didn't talk to

people so much as she scorched their immediate vicinity.

But let us make no mistake about this. Beatrice Arthur's memorable portrayal of what had to be the most unrestrained and intense telemom ever to burst through a picture tube was a breakthrough for its sheer level of maternal chutzpah. Maude was not a woman who shrank from any sort of challenge, and *Maude* was not a show that had much trouble leaping over and through some previously shackled social barriers and bolted content doors.

Consider that over the course of the series, Maude had an abortion (in a highly contentious episode that drew heavy protests), had a hysterectomy, underwent a facelift, went through menopause, battled alcoholism, saw a UFO and started a campaign to get actor Henry Fonda elected president of the United States (a goal that called Maude's mental health into question). Moreover, her husband Walter (Bill Macy) had an even more severe battle with booze, enduring a bankruptcy and a nervous breakdown.

Until Lear had the guts with *Maude* to pierce the taboos associated with portraying middle age in America, TV moms were still reasonably docile sorts, more attuned to baking cookies than creating controversy. It was highly original—if totally jarring—to suddenly have a brassy broad like Maude in our faces every week. It was almost unprecedented: a mother on TV, experiencing real life—on her terms.

As one might expect, Maude's motherly skills were similar to her social ones: coarse and decidedly unsubtle. She lived in suburban Tuckahoe, New York, with Walter (husband number four, no surprise) and her divorced twenty-seven-year-old daughter Carol (Adrienne Barbeau). Maude also employed a housekeeper (she went through three of them, one at a time).

Maude did her best to try to conduct Carol's life for her, particularly as it grew apparent that Carol wasn't very good at running it herself. Theirs was, thus, a contentious relationship, though one that did not lack for love. Maude had more than her share of faults, but she was always there for her daughter—perhaps even more regularly than that daughter would have preferred.

Even at her most parentally-challenged, Maude was never less than colorfully caustic. It's the kind of stuff of which legendary TV moms are made.

Classic Mom-ents

After learning that her daughter Carol is in clinical therapy, Maude confronts the psychiatrist as being a waste of time, energy, and money. But before long, the therapist has Maude recalling experiences with her own domineering mother.

Maude discovers that, at age forty-seven, she's pregnant. She faces an agonizing decision over whether or not to carry the child to term. Maude vacilates between wanting a child versus her suitability as a mother, given her advancing age. She would ultimately decide on an abortion.

♀ When Maude criticizes husband Walter for his out-of-control boozing, the argument turns violent and Walter gives his wife a black eye. Only when her daughter Carol and grandson Phillip decide to move out does Walter finally begin to take seriously the fact he has a problem with alcohol. Maude's courage and character in refusing to back down to an irrational husband in need of help inspires Carol.

♀ Fancying herself a modern, liberated mother, Maude finds her supposed emancipated beliefs getting a thorough test when Carol invites her boyfriend to spend the night in her bedroom (under her mother's roof).

♀ Maude can see clearly that Carol is about to make a huge mistake after her daughter falls for a legally separated man with a womanizing reputation. But when Maude warns Carol that getting involved with the guy isn't such a good idea, she's attacked as a "meddling mother," and Carol decides it may be time to move out.

♀ With Carol engaged to marry Chris (Fred Grandy) in eight months, Maude puts a down payment on a new home for the couple. But to Carol's horror, the house turns out to be directly across the street from Maude and Walter.

"You can't expect me to have lunch with a man whose favorite part of a chicken is the right wing."
—Maude

Olivia Walton (Michael Learned)

The Waltons

(Sept. 14, 1972 to Nov. 29, 1980), CBS

There was never any question of who was in charge when Olivia Walton was around. Known as "Mama" to her tribe of seven kids, she tolerated no foolishness from the brood. If they were going to live under her roof, then they would have to abide by her God-fearing, moralistic

credo and do their chores without any grumbling. She was firm, but her kids always knew where they stood in the pecking order: below her.

Being one of Olivia's children carried with it both great advantages and disadvantages as their life script played itself out in *The Waltons*. They got to lead a simple, rural life in a breathtaking Blue Ridge Mountain region of Jefferson County, Virginia. They were blessed with a reassuring dose of discipline and direction. And they got to be part of a large tightly-knit family.

On the down side, these kids had to be bored silly. Some occasional tedium, however, was a small price to pay for all of that down-home wisdom. That's certainly the way *The Waltons* made it appear, anyway.

Nonetheless, *The Waltons* proved to be a major hit for CBS throughout the 1970s, playing for nine seasons and standing as one of the most gentle dramas ever to grace network TV. It was based on creator Earl Hamner Jr.'s reminiscences of his own childhood, one bereft of any of society's corruptive influences. Hamner's show was all warmth and positive values to the occasional point of nausea.

Olivia (played with great passion by Michael Learned) and husband John (Ralph Waite) presided over a household that included kids John Boy (Richard Thomas and later Robert Wightman), Mary Ellen (Judy Norton-Taylor), Jim-Bob (David W. Harper), Elizabeth (Kami Cotler), Jason (Jon Walmsley), Erin (Mary Elizabeth McDonough), and Ben (Eric Scott).

While she demanded respect and ruled with something of an iron fist, Olivia displayed a vast nurturing side as well. But the woman also suffered as few TV moms have suffered before. She endured polio, tuberculosis, a stay in a sanitarium, a horrific fire, the ravages of the Great Depression, and sending her boys off to fight in World War II. It wasn't an easy life. But Olivia remained religious and uncommonly upbeat through all of the travails, and even appeared to grow more liberated in her thinking in the process.

Television moms simply do not come any tougher.

Classic Mom-ents

Olivia Walton is taken ill one Sunday in February after church. It is determined that she has polio, traumatizing her husband John and seven children. The family refuses to believe that Olivia will never walk again and provides her with immediate and overwhelming support to help pull her through.

After taking a job as a door-to-door salesperson, Olivia discovers that she is again pregnant. Initially, daughter Elizabeth is resentful, feeling she will be displaced in the Walton family structure. But Lizzie and her siblings all grow attached to the idea of a new baby. Unfortunately, Olivia miscarries.

While driving to visit a friend, the truck carrying Olivia, Elizabeth, and Jim-Bob is disabled by a flat tire. As the blowout occurs, the truck crashes into a bush and a hen they were taking escapes. All three chase the hen into the woods, growing disoriented and lost as a storm brews overhead. A search party is summoned to track down the missing Waltons while Olivia uses all of her motherly skills to keep everyone in the group hopeful and alert.

A raging fire destroys most of the Walton home as well as a portion of a novel that John Boy had written and planned to submit to a publishing company. Olivia works hard to keep the family together in the wake of the disaster. But she and John ultimately decide it best for the children to stay with friends and neighbors.

Olivia grows excited at the prospect of a famed evangelist coming to visit Walton's Mountain. She prays that John will take part in a meeting with the pastor and agree to be baptized. John attends the meeting at his wife's behest but bolts out the door as soon as the preacher begins his "fire and brimstone" diatribe. Olivia comes to accept John's decision, seeing him as a "searcher."

After she and John return home from a vacation, Olivia discovers some devastating news: she is suffering from tuberculosis and must enter a sanitarium if she is ever to recover. Her children are inconsolable, remaining so throughout an extremely trying year on Walton's Mountain.

"If you want to please someone a lot, one way is to let them teach you how to read even when you already know how."
—Olivia Walton

Florida Evans *(Esther Rolle)*

Good Times
(Feb. 1, 1974 to Aug. 1, 1979), CBS

Those who are old enough to remember the urban comedy *Good Times* will recall it as the show that quickly came to be dominated by Jimmie Walker as the jive-talking, insincere, and over-confident eldest son J.J. His regular blurting of the catchphrase "dy-no-mite" became a peculiar battle cry of the mid-1970s.

Recalled perhaps less well, but infinitely more fondly, was the dignified presence of Esther Rolle as the proud and joyous Florida Evans. She was the rock-solid wife of James Evans (John Amos during the show's first two seasons) and the mother to over-the-top, seventeen-year-old J.J., sixteen-year-old Thelma (BerNadette Stanis), and ten-year-old Michael (Ralph Carter).

That Florida stood as a strong and sensitive pillar of wisdom in the Evans' lower-middle-class home on Chicago's South Side was a given; what made her that much more special was the masterful grasp Rolle had of the character. She was Florida, at least as far

89

as her value system and the clarity of her righteous moral message.

Despite living in a ghetto with three willful kids and a husband who was perpetually out of work, Florida persevered and thrived. She probably had it tougher than did any mom figure in the history of telemothering. Yet she never lost either her sense of humor or her focus in keeping food on the table for those kids.

This was just a great lady, whether we're talking about Rolle or her alter ego. Florida always managed to be available for her family and rarely allowed her station in life to have a bearing on how she carried—or felt about—herself. And that honorability trickled down to her kids. Except for J.J., of course. Rolle demonstrated her own sense of values when she quit *Good Times* for the entire 1977–78 season (returning the following year) after becoming disenchanted with the jive-talking role model provided by J.J. that had come to dominate the show.

It's surely unfortunate that the Norman Lear-produced *Good Times* came to be identified almost solely with Walker's

dopey antics. J.J. aside, the show was one of the richest and boldest black-themed comedies ever to air. As is the Lear trademark, it wasn't afraid to take chances, dealing with topics like armed robbery and giving an edgy depiction of ghetto life at a time when it simply wasn't done.

The show had the distinction of being a series spinoff of a series spinoff. It began its life as *All in the Family*, which begat *Maude*, which begat *Good Times*. Florida actually started out as a recurring player on *All in the Family* and then jumped to *Maude* as a regular, portraying Maude's housekeeper.

On *Good Times*, the times were good only because Florida made it so with her positive attitude. Even when her husband "died" with Amos' decision to leave the show, she carried on stoically and often even with great humor despite her trauma. And the woman held her family together with a passion borne of determination that we could see emanated from her very soul.

That, ladies and gentlemen, is acting.

Classic Mom-ents

♀ James finds a brown paper bag containing $65,000 in cash, having been tossed into an alley during a botched supermarket holdup. He insists on keeping the money, but Florida wouldn't hear of it. What sort of example would that set for the kids?

♂ J.J. proves himself to be poor at following examples, anyway. When he lacks the money to purchase needed art supplies, he holds up a liquor store on his eighteenth birthday. Florida is left in a state of near nervous collapse, wondering where she went wrong with the boy. J.J.'s excuse fails to reassure her.

♀ James is present when J.J. is shot and wounded as a result of gang crossfire. As soon as he knows that J.J. is all right, James is hellbent on hunting down the punk who shot his boy. But Florida, ever the voice of reason, assures her enraged husband that if they don't sit back and wait for the gunman to be arrested, the damage from the bullet would worsen.

♂ A young woman hires J.J. to paint her nude portrait, posing inside the Evans apartment. Florida begs to differ and insists that the woman at least put on a bathing suit to cover up…well…a few places. A compromise is struck.

♂ Florida invites a neighbor to dinner after Michael notices dog food cans in her garbage can out back, which is odd because the woman has no dog. When she brings over meatloaf to serve as a main course, both Florida and Michael are left to wonder if there is any dog food in it.

"James, there is dignity in all work. It's not the kind of work you do that gives you dignity, it's how good you do it."
—Florida Evans

91

Caroline Ingalls (*Karen Grassle*)

Little House on the Prairie

(Sept. 11, 1974 to March 21, 1982), NBC

In this phenomenally successful frontier drama series based on the *Little House* books by Laura Ingalls Wilder, Michael Landon—in the

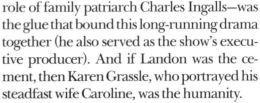

role of family patriarch Charles Ingalls—was the glue that bound this long-running drama together (he also served as the show's executive producer). And if Landon was the cement, then Karen Grassle, who portrayed his steadfast wife Caroline, was the humanity.

Little House on the Prairie was actually a nighttime soap masquerading as a family period piece. Upheaval was a constant. Families went broke. Some children went blind, while others miraculously regained their sight. Schools burned to the ground. Alcoholism exacted its usual toll.

Through it all, one homestead family persevered back in the 1870s and 1880s, carving out a harsh but satisfying living on a small farm near Walnut Grove, Minnesota. The Ingalls clan didn't have much in the way of worldly possessions, but they made up for it in love and support. Caroline had become the mother to eight children (five natural and three adopted) by the time the series was done.

Yes indeed, Caroline was a busy TV mom. And as if having all of those mouths to feed and bodies to clothe were not enough, the woman grew bored with her role of housewife and took a job outside the home as a restaurant

cook (and a particularly noteworthy one at that). Caroline was hailed, in fact, as the greatest down-home cook in all of Walnut Grove.

But that would all end when the Ingalls family fell on particularly hard times and had to up and move again, a development that happened every few years or so. But Caroline was a stoic marvel. No matter how bad things got, she almost never made a fuss or complained. And what does this mom do when her family runs up against some really hard luck? She adopts another kid!

Is this lady a hero or what? Caroline was the ultimate support system, always available to prop up her husband or give those kids a much-needed squeeze. If she were forced to relinquish a few of her own dreams and desires to make sure her family never wanted for a thing, well, that was a sacrifice this TV mom was more than willing to make.

Might Caroline Ingalls have been something of a martyr, even maybe a glutton for punishment (given her penchant for taking in more kids as her situation grew more grim)? Maybe. But back in the late 1800s, that's just what a mother did. And when mom is able to raise a perfect little pigtailed princess like Laura (series narrator Melissa Gilbert), you don't ask questions. You just let her be mom.

Classic Mom-ents

♀ Caroline gives advice to Grace Edwards (Bonnie Bartlett) and to daughter Laura about ways they can make the males they like jealous so they will ask the girls to the spring dance. When it turns out to be a faulty strategy, Caroline instructs them both to come clean.

♀ When Caroline slices her leg on a loose wire from the wagon, the cut festers as she stays behind to bake pies for a church gathering. The infection worsens, making her fevered and delusional to the point where Caroline believes she should perform her own surgery. She makes an incision in her leg to drain the poison. Yet even in her state of near-delirium, her maternal instincts drive

Caroline as she mumbles a driving need to "survive for the children."

♀ While husband Charles is away, Caroline hires a young, strapping handyman to do repairs around the house. The man falls in love with her and Caroline finds herself attracted to him as well. She finally tells this lust object that he must leave.

♀ Caroline becomes pregnant, and she so badly wants a boy that she drives everyone nuts with her constant references to the baby as "him." Charles decides to send the girls away so he can be alone with his wife when the baby arrives. And once again, she gives birth to a girl. But after she sees her new daughter, Caroline is fully accepting of her gender.

♀ As Caroline accompanies Charles to their high school reunion, they grow sullen upon discovering that most of their friends in school have become rich. But upon further investigation, the Ingalls duo finds that despite the money, none of their rich old gang is especially happy. They ultimately realize it is they who are rich, since their family members love one another.

"I believe it was the watermelon that caused the fever 'n ague (malaria)."
—Caroline Ingalls

94

Marion Cunningham (*Marion Ross*)
Happy Days
(Jan. 15, 1974 to July 12, 1984), ABC

As 1950s TV moms go, Marion Cunningham came equipped with tons of edge. Maybe that's because she showed up not in the '50s but in the '70s as the prototype warm and gracious neighborhood ma on *Happy Days*. By the time Mrs. C., as she was called by everyone, showed up on the scene, June Cleaver and Donna Stone and Margaret Anderson had all come and gone. Telemotherhood, 1950s style, was Marion's to reinvent. And so she did.

Not that Mrs. C. (portrayed by the extraordinary Marion Ross) was such an outward rebel. She was still pretty straight and wholesome and mostly deferential (to roly-poly hubby Howard, played by Tom Bosley). She did her share of milk and cookies and preached morality to keep son Richie (Ron Howard), daughter Joanie (Erin Moran), and pals Potsie (Anson Williams), Ralph Malph (Donny Most), Chachi (Scott Baio), and especially Fonzie (Henry Winkler) on the straight-and-narrow path.

But Mrs. C. was at heart a feisty babe who let her wants and needs be known. She had an independent streak that prevented any of that suffering-in-silence nonsense. When she was irked, there was never any doubt—and we loved the lady for it.

Think about it: Not only

95

Fonz let down his hair for her and only her.

This was no small feat. The Fonz never ceded control of his actions or his physical space to anybody, but Mrs. C. was different. He respected the woman. If anyone dared insult Mrs. C., Fonzie would make them pay. And to be sure, we always suspected that the lady had a very special place in her heart for Fonz. Despite the limitations of being a '50s telemom operating on a '70s show, Ross inflected the character with more sheer spunk and independence than was evident in the majority of her motherly ilk.

Mrs. C. simply made everyone in her world feel as if she were their own mother. She fussed over friends and ac-

did Mrs. C. give birth to Richie and thereby present America with the ultimate all-American kid, she also proved to be the only human on the planet who could tame the wild beast that was the leather-jacketed biker dude, The Fonz. We sensed that Marion always carried a silent torch for the guy, and he for her. They danced together. They flirted. quaintances alike as if they were special. The fact that Richie himself was such an innocent, such a—let's just go right out and say it—a wimp, had little to do with his old lady. A mother can only do so much; nature is responsible for the rest. In Marion, TV gave us a mother who went way beyond the housecleaning and brownie baking required of the job; she was the essence of nurturing and vigilance itself. A TV mom among TV moms.

Classic Mom-ents

♀ Howard brings an old Army buddy named Fred Washington home for a visit prior to Fred's getting married. A neighbor comes in to use the phone and is somewhat aghast to meet Fred, who is black. Aghast at the prejudice in their midst, Marion suggests to husband Howard that Fred's wedding be held in their home. Howard agrees.

♀ When Howard begs out of being her dance partner at the annual Harvest Moon Dance Contest, Marion asks Fonzie if he would enter the contest with her. He agrees, and they team up for the tango to great applause. It shows that when Marion puts her mind to something—whether it be baking a cake or dancing in a competition—she follows through.

♀ Frustrated and bored with her life, Marion lands a job as a waitress at Al's diner. Marion proceeds to take over the joint, criticizing the menu and seizing control of things. Fonzie orders Richie to fire his own mother. She begins sobbing in the kitchen. Howard is left to reassure his wife that she's not a failure in any way, and Marion registers for music school.

♀ Marion fears that she is growing old and that Howard is eyeing younger women. After a chat with Fonzie, she tries something different to entice her husband, serving dinner in an Arabian princess outfit. After Marion breaks down in tears, Howard tells her he is very happily married and would never leave her for a younger woman. They head upstairs for some time alone.

♀ When everyone gathers at the Cunninghams' to watch a football game on Thanksgiving Day, Marion fears they have lost the meaning of the holiday. In a dream sequence, it's the 1600s and all of the Happy Days regulars are Pilgrims. They wind up inviting the Indians to their Thanksgiving feast. Back in real time, Marion finishes her story, and all emerge feeling thankful.

♀ Marion insists that she and Howard renew their vows on their twenty-fifth wedding anniversary, but Howard admits to feeling "silly" about getting married all over again. Howard goes along with it anyway, "proposes" to Marion again, and they marry a second time. It underscores Marion's dedication to her husband and to her family.

"And then you . . . your father didn't have . . . time to get a wedding ring so he slipped a . . . little peppermint Life Saver on my finger."
——Mrs. C

Phyllis Lindstrom
(Cloris Leachman)

Phyllis
(Sept. 8, 1975 to Aug. 30, 1977), CBS

Phyllis was the second spin-off of *The Mary Tyler Moore Show* to get its own spot in primetime, the other having been *Rhoda*. In *Phyllis*, Cloris Leachman continued to inhabit the character she had played for five years on *MTM*, Phyllis Lindstrom—the neighbor, friend, and landlady of Mary Richards in Minneapolis. For the new show, Phyllis moved back home to San Francisco following the death of her husband, Lars.

The series earned impressive ratings during its short two-season run despite being hit with some grim hurdles. Barbara Colby, the actress originally cast to portray Phyllis' boss Julie Erskine at the photography studio that employed her, was brutally murdered by gangbangers in a drive-by shooting soon after production began. Liz Torres would replace her.

Then while *Phyllis* moved through its second year on CBS, the elderly actors who played the roles of Mother Dexter and Arthur Lanson—Judith Lowry and Burt

Mustin—died within a few months of one another (she in December 1976, he the following February).

Those setbacks, more than the show's quality, contributed to an undeservedly abbreviated run for *Phyllis*. In it, Phyllis moved to the Bay Area with her teen daughter Bess (Lisa Gerritsen), living with her late husband's ditzy mother Audrey (Jane Rose), and Audrey's second husband, Judge Jonathan Dexter (Henry Jones). Before long, Judge Dexter's elderly, sarcasm-spewing mother (Lowry) had moved herself into the house as well.

Phyllis didn't much alter her behavior from the tone she set on *Mary Tyler Moore*. She remained self-absorbed and insensitive, trying to mind the business of everyone around her and often neglecting to take care of her own. That made her a motherly challenge for daughter Bess, who was often put in the position of bailing her clueless mom out of socially dicey situations.

Yet while Phyllis may have possessed a peculiar sense of how she came across to the outside world, there was never any question about her devotion to Bess. It was total, even if her daughter might have appreciated a little bit less unconditional attention and more genuine guidance. The two of them bonded in their mutual dysfunction, generally over relationships with men.

Phyllis intruded, overstepped boundaries, smothered, and pretty much made a nuisance of herself. But isn't that what moms are for? Leachman played the meddling matron to the hilt, and it was a hoot. It's only regrettable that she didn't get a chance to keep Phyllis around a little longer.

Classic Mom-ents

♀ Phyllis believes that her relationship with her teenage daughter, Bess, is stagnating and figures they need to spend more time together. So she asks her daughter out to a dance club, where the two of them stay up all night telling one another deep, dark secrets.

♀ Bess announces she has become engaged to be married, and Phyllis believes her daughter to be too young to wed. She invites the parents of the would-be groom over for dinner—only to discover they are dwarfs. The three wind up becoming fast friends.

♀ After Bess dumps her boyfriend, the guy falls in love with Phyllis, who isn't quite sure how to handle the situation. Should she tell her daughter? Should she be offended? Should she feel flattered yet remain silent? She finally decides to make an issue of it and tell Bess as a means of motherly protection,

since reconciliation with the guy might now prove a bad idea.

♀ Bess and her classmates start a riot when they hear that one of their teachers was fired because she posed nude many years before. After Bess gets expelled from school for her behavior, Phyllis decides to intercede and get her daughter reinstated.

♀ Phyllis goes on a trip with friends. While away, she calls home early one morning and hears a male voice pick up the phone. She freaks and demands to have it out with Bess right then and there. But when Phyllis arrives home, her worst fears are not confirmed. Her daughter wasn't sleeping with a strange guy in her home after all. But Bess is nonetheless disturbed by mom's meddling.

"What a wonderful child you are, Bess. I must be a wonderful mother."
—Phyllis

Louise "Weezy" Jefferson (Isabel Sanford)

The Jeffersons
(Jan. 18, 1975 to July 23, 1985), CBS

Few TV series spin-offs have proven as successful as was *The Jeffersons*, which creator-producer Norman Lear spun from his legendary *All in the Family*. George and Louise Jefferson were Archie Bunker's married neighbors in a working-class area of Queens. Then his small dry cleaning business blossomed into a seven-store chain. So the Jeffersons pulled up stakes and moved to a fancy high-rise on Manhattan's swank Upper East Side.

It was at that point that George (Sher-

the Family, featuring George as a wealthy, blustery black man and a counterpoint to the working-class white bigot, Archie Bunker.

Throughout its run, *The Jeffersons* remained a hot-button comedy that wasn't afraid to play the race card from a different perspective (that of a rich guy working to move his head out of the ghetto even as his body sat in a penthouse). George was the quick-tempered, wildly opinionated and tactless one; Louise was the low-key, warmhearted one. Their impulsive son Lionel (played by Mike Evans and later Damon Evans) fell someplace in between.

Weezy was likewise careful not to let the Jeffersons' sudden wealth go to her head, as it already had with full-fledged snob George. Louise supplied a filter of earthy humanity that counteracted her blowhard, intolerant husband of thirty years. Whereas George railed against everything including Lionel's choice of a mixed-race spouse, Louise tended to be extraordinarily accepting.

That was indeed the way Louise consis-

man Hemsley) and Louise, or "Weezy" (Isabel Sanford), leaped from *All in the Family* into their own show that would chart their lives just as they were "movin' on up," as the Jeffersons theme song intoned. Their sitcom became an institution in its own right, building slowly and finally cracking the ratings Top 10 in its fifth season and remaining in the Top 20 for five seasons running.

The Jeffersons would stick around for ten years in all and make stars of Hemsley, Sanford, and Marla Gibbs, who portrayed their sarcasm-spewing maid Florence. The show supplied a brilliant contrast to *All in*

tently conducted herself as a telemom of some repute. She was more apt to shield Lionel from George than to discipline him, which wasn't necessarily an effective way to parent. But she had little choice.

In fact, George needed the maternal discipline more than his son did. But he received plenty of it from his own old lady Mother Jefferson (Zara Cully) and of course from Florence, who looked at George as a bag needing to be punched.

There was little for Louise to do in a motherly way except to be sweet and supportive. She accomplished this with a rare stamina that painted her as one of the tube's all-time greats.

Classic Mom-ents

♀ Louise Jefferson insists that—for the sake of their son Lionel, if nothing else—she and husband George keep both of their feet planted in their modest past even as they adapt to living a more wealthy lifestyle. George is incensed that his wife would invite some of their old Harlem friends to dinner on the same night he's entertaining a high-society businessman. Louise shrugs and implores her husband to get over himself.

♂ It's high school graduation day for Louise and George's son, Lionel. Unfortunately, in Lionel's case the "high" part has a double meaning. He has smoked a joint and gotten himself stoned prior to the ceremony. Louise's response is to make sure George doesn't find out, for the good of humanity.

♀ Neither Louise nor George is terribly thrilled when Lionel breaks the news that he's moving into his own apartment. But they are even more upset upon finding out that their son's new roommate will be his girlfriend (and soon to be fiancée and wife), Jenny (Berlinda Tolbert).

♀ When Lionel begins strutting around with a playboy attitude, Louise finds herself greatly distressed. George, of course, loves the idea that his son is finally acting like a guy with money. Louise is forced to give the boy a good talking-to, though, when he lets it slip that he's now considering quitting college. That would be permissible only over his mother's dead body.

♀ Louise encourages George to secretly defy Lionel and Jenny by entering their granddaughter Jessica (Ebonie Smith) in a baby beauty contest. To make matters worse, they misplace Jessica in the process. It is an act of meddling and irresponsibility that is beneath Louise but entirely consistent for her husband.

"You best keep those eyeballs in that head or you're gonna be movin' on down, George Jefferson!"
—Louise Jefferson

Abby Bradford
(Betty Buckley)

Eight is Enough
(March 15, 1977 to Aug. 29, 1981), ABC

While *Eight is Enough* was not quite the edgiest show in television history, the comedy-drama had just enough bite to rise above the level of total fluff. And a big part of that juice was the presence of Betty Buckley as Abby Bradford, a pretty schoolteacher who may just have been the bravest TV mom ever to grace primetime.

What made her so brave? Simply the fact that she would agree to marry a man (Tom Bradford, played by Dick Van Patten) with eight children and become stepmother to a clan of independent offspring ages eight to twenty-three who had lost their mother only a year before. That takes industrial-strength nerve. It's like marrying nine people in a world where getting betrothed to just one is a challenge.

It all happened pretty suddenly for Abby. In the *Eight is Enough* storyline, Joan Bradford—Tom's wife of twenty-five years and mother to the brood—succumbed to an undisclosed illness. Writing Joan's character out of the show was necessitated by the death of the actress who portrayed her, Diana Hyland, after just four episodes. Initially, it was noted simply that Joan was "away." By the following fall, the story noted that she had died.

So Buckley (and, by extension, Abby) had to get focused in a hurry to fill in on such a new and vulnerable show. It is to the actress' supreme credit that she was able to make a potential awkward transition appear so smooth and seamless.

During the show's four-and-a-half-year run on ABC, Abby would evolve from tentative (during her brief courtship with Tom) to oversensitive (working hard to be sure it didn't appear to the kids as if she were trying to replace their mother in their hearts) to involved and caring (once she got her sea legs in the Bradford household). Abby had met Tom when she came to the family home to tutor one of the youngsters; by November of the same year, she would be going to the altar with her new husband.

Abby earned her doctorate in education as the show moved along and started work as a counselor at the local high school and privately in homes as well. Inside her own house, she would enjoy close, special relationships with several of the Bradford kids—particularly fifteen-year-old Elizabeth (Connie Needham), fourteen-year-old Tommy (Willie Aames), and the family baby, eight-year-old Nicholas (Adam Rich). The other Bradfords—all of whom were at least of voting age—included Nancy (Dianne Kay), Susan (Susan Richardson), Joannie (Laurie Walters), Mary (Lani O'Grady), and David (Grant Goodeve).

In *Eight Is Enough*, the still-traumatized kids were always searching for the chink in Abby's armor, the imperfection that would expose her as a fraud. They never found it. Abby proved to be the superior human being who was necessary for the job: trusting, loyal, sensitive, available, and ever-aware of boundaries.

Yes, stepmoms can be great TV moms, too.

Classic Mom-ents

🕴 Elizabeth admits to her stepmother Abby that she is sexually active with her boyfriend, and Abby makes arrangements to help her acquire birth control pills. This greatly distresses Tom, who believes it will only encourage behavior of which he does not approve. A battle of ideologies ensues.

🕴 Abby's parenting skills are put to the test when stepson Tommy comes home drunk. She decides to play it cool until the appropriate way of dealing with the situation becomes clear: discussing it with him alone, without Tommy's seven siblings or his father nearly. Abby's discretion and sensitivity would diffuse the problem—and win the teenager's instant trust.

🕴 When Elizabeth is excluded from her high school graduation ceremonies after she takes part in a dangerous senior prank, Abby is inspired to intercede on the girl's behalf—taking her case to the school administration to have the decision reversed.

♀ The Bradford kids, now older and in possession of driver's licenses, try to make Abby feel guilty over the fact she never shares her ultra-cool MG sports car with the family. They all want to drive it. But she lets it be known that some things can involve no compromise.

♀ Tom and his daughter Susan grow increasingly upset when Abby spends what they see as too much time with Susan's new boyfriend. The situation turns out to be innocent enough—they simply have much in common and enjoy one another's company—but it teaches Abby an important telemothering lesson: appearances, no matter how deceiving, can breed misunderstanding and resentment if not addressed immediately.

"What makes you think we're the typical all-American family?"
—Abby Bradford

𝓜ork *(Robin Williams)*

Mork & Mindy

(Sept. 14, 1978 to June 10, 1982), ABC

It's obvious to discern that Mork, an alien from the planet Ork, is not your average TV mom. After being assigned by the Orkan leader Orson to cover Earth as part of his intergalactic exploration, Mork met and fell for an earthling named Mindy (Pam Dawber). They got married. They parented a child. But it didn't happen in what one might view as a conventional way.

No, Mork didn't do anything in a typical manner. Why should having a kid be any different? Of course, it was Mork's alter ego

Robin Williams who made the space visitor so eccentrically memorable during the four-season run of this comedy that spun from an episode of *Happy Days*. On that show, Mork had landed on Earth and attempted to kidnap Richie Cunningham (Ron Howard).

The warped character was such a smash in his single appearance that ABC realized it had to give Williams his own series. And so *Mork & Mindy* was born solely as a vehicle to allow Williams the weekly chance to mug, ad-lib, mock, imitate, and otherwise leap all over the screen as a one-man comedy frenzy.

Television had never seen the likes of someone as manic and uncontainable as was Williams during the early days of *Mork &*

Mindy. Both he and the show would lose some of the wacky flair during its second and third seasons as the show searched for stories with more bite and meaning. The audience didn't want that. They wanted slapstick. That sense would return in season four when Mork and Mindy became parents.

Here's how it worked: as was the custom with Orkans who have mated (and unbeknownst to Mindy), Mork ejected a small egg from his navel. The egg grew larger until it cracked open and out popped a fully grown, 225-pound, middle-aged adult male they named Mearth (portrayed by Williams' idol, the great Jonathan Winters). Mearth looked like an adult in his fifties but still babbled baby talk. Since things grow backward on Ork, Mearth would gradually grow younger rather than older and die while still an infant.

This, of course, allowed for some uncomfortable moments for Mork and his wife here on Earth, where preschools tend to frown on toddlers who resemble grandparents. But somehow it worked out, and Mork adapted quickly to "motherhood" (since Mork ejected the egg, it was he who carried the maternal role). He was protective and doting and predictably neurotic.

There would be several factors fueling Mork's motherly anxiety. In a short time, Mearth was kidnapped by a cult, rejected by his schoolmates as "different," held hostage by a computer, and spoiled rotten by his mother (Mork). But Mork meant well, bonded with the boy, and loved Mearth as only a mother with a middle-aged toddler can.

Yes, it was wacky stuff. But it left Mork with another dimension to his complex persona—illustrating that telemoms come in all shapes, personalities, genders, and planetary affiliations.

Classic Mom-ents

♀ Mindy proves to be less than accepting of the new 225-pound son she has inexplicably helped bring into the world—and who calls her "Shoe." This hurts Mork's feelings terribly. Mork decides to take drastic measures to help Mindy bond with Mearth, leaving them alone together in the studio at her TV station.

♂ Mork feels like a total failure as a parent because Mearth idolizes Superman—who has two jobs—while Mork stays home raising his son and therefore has no other employment. Then Mearth finds Mork's spacesuit and asks if he is a superhero. Mork slips into the "crime fighter" suit and heads for a seedy bar in search of bad guys.

♂ When Mork sees Mearth crying because a dog has eaten his toy aircraft, he decides to spend a fortune buying the "boy" presents to assure Mearth's happiness. Mindy insists he return all of the gifts so as not to spoil their kid, leaving Mork to explain to Mearth that his imagination is his most precious gift.

♀ An incident convinces Mork and Mindy that they must tell Mearth he is half alien and not like the other kids. Mork assures his son that he is aging backward and will eventually look like Earth children, but Mearth wants to go to Ork and runs away. Instead, Mearth is kidnapped by a utopian cult.

♂ A short circuit switches Mork's mind with his son Mearth's on the night that Mindy's new boss wants to meet the employees' families. The mind transfer forces Mindy to take Mearth in Mork's body to the gathering with the boss.

"Nanu, Nanu."
——Mork

~3~

The 1980s
In Search of Paradise

By 1980, some 70 percent of American women with children were doing at least some work outside the home. So it was incumbent on network TV to reflect this reality. And it did—to a degree.

Suddenly, TV moms were no longer trapped inside the house spouting platitudes and niceties at the kids. Instead, they were barking at their latchkey offspring or talking down to them between office meetings. Other mothers, like Nancy Weston (Patricia Wettig) of *thirtysomething*, found a way to stress out even without the weight of conventional full-time employment.

And then there was Peg Bundy (Katey Sagal) of *Married...With Children*. She never found the time to do much of anything. She didn't have a job, never cooked, never cleaned, and rarely got up from the sofa even to discipline the kids (who more or less raised themselves). Peg apparently wasn't even motivated in the bedroom. But she nonetheless supplied a gift to the American TV viewer, embodying a worst-case scenario against which all other telemoms would be measured into eternity.

Peg, however, was not the rule in the 1980s, nor was the all-wise, all-everything Clair Huxtable (Phylicia Rashad) of *The Cosby Show*. Clair represented the high end of the 1980s mom scale, Peg the bottom. In between, the image of the TV mom was undergoing a quiet transition that would find mother characters falling more or less into four camps: thirty-something white-collar professionals (Clair; Elyse Keaton of *Family Ties*); thirtyish blue-collar working stiffs (Roseanne Conner of *Roseanne*); big-mouth older moms (Sophia Petrillo of *The Golden Girls*); and angst-riddled homemakers harboring a need to bust out (*thirtysomething's* Nancy; Norma Arnold of *The Wonder Years*).

If TV of the 1980s finally shed for good its staid, antiquated and one-dimensional idea of what constitutes an American mother, the decade would likewise reflect the ways in which moms were growing a bit more self-focused. That ideal naturally mirrored what was going on in society at large. Yet it nonetheless proved occasionally jarring, given the previous makeup of the telemothering universe.

It has to be remembered that aside from the occasional Maude Findlay, Florida Evans, Louise Jefferson, or Marion Cunningham, TV moms up until the 1980s were designed to be human yield signs—never insisting on their own right of way. They were, as a group, professional deferrers. If their wants and needs dovetailed with those of their husbands and kids, great; if not, they were programmed to swallow their desires and live contentedly through the needs of their loved ones. It was an admirable way to go through life, if generally not a fulfilling one.

But with the '80s emerged the possibility that telemoms maybe could have it all. They could have the loving husband and the well-adjusted offspring and not be consumed exclusively with lives of housework and meatloaf recipes. They could work out-

side their homes and reveal feelings of independence without evoking any sense of rebellion or selfishness. And at the same time, their husbands could share the household and childcare duties without seeming like henpecked wimps.

Heck, TV moms suddenly didn't even necessarily need to have husbands at all. One of the more radical examples of this notion was supplied by a lady named Murphy Brown (Candice Bergen). She would join the TV fray before the 1980s were through, though Murph didn't become an actual mom until May 1992. And while the mother wasn't lacking for father or husband volunteers, Murphy opted to fly solo.

The fact she even had an option represented a new wrinkle in TV's motherly equation.

There was indeed a feeling that for the television mom, this was a decade of real transition. TV's focus had yet to fully catch up to this new era of mother character choice. A few, like Elyse Keaton and Nancy Weston, appeared to be hopelessly stuck in between their responsibilities to family and self and never quite reconciled it. Others, like Clair Huxtable, were simply too self-assured to give the issue a lot of thought.

But conflicted realities aside, the '80s were also the time when TV moms finally started to get a few real punch lines tossed their way. This was surely true of Estelle Getty, who received most of the wisecracks through her elderly alter ego Sophia on *Golden Girls*. (It was said on the show that Sophia had suffered a stroke that destroyed the "tact" cells in her brain.)

The decade would finally close out with an irony: it took TV a mere eighteen extra years to finally get 1960s motherhood right. The vehicle was *The Wonder Years*, which arrived on the scene in 1988; the TV mom was Norma Arnold (played to perfection by Alley Mills), a stay-at-home, bread-baking mommy living in 1968 suburbia with her gruff, tortured working-class husband and three strong-willed kids.

Norma hoped and prayed that her joyless existence could one day rise to match her rose-colored optimism. But the look of defeat in her eyes told us that she knew better. She also never allowed her silent agony to interfere with living for her kids—which meant often shielding them from a distant and demanding father.

It was just Norma Arnold's misfortune that she wasn't able to raise her kids twenty years later, because the 1980s could well have brought her a long overdue liberation of the soul. It surely seemed to do the trick for that decade's collection of TV moms.

The legacy of the '80s telemom was ultimately that of stepping stone. She paved the way to a new maternal reality in which choice and flexibility grew from a pipe dream into the norm. A whole new set of pitfalls resulted that called into question the concept of televised motherhood itself. Was she now an independent soul? A more well-rounded nurturer? An uncertain explorer? A little bit of all three? All that remained obvious was that a corner had been turned and there could be no turning back because with the coming of the 1990s, all previous rules were about to be obliterated.

Eleanor Southworth ("Miss Ellie") Ewing

(Barbara Bel Geddes)

Dallas

(April 2, 1978 to May 3, 1991), CBS

As the well-heeled matriarch of the cutthroat gang hanging out at the South-fork Ranch, Miss Ellie Ewing may go down as the most dysfunctional TV mom ever. She was to her TV ilk what Rose Kennedy was to political matriarchs: ageless, regal, graceful, powerful, prideful, courageous and—to be sure—indestructible. The woman kept right on ticking despite taking more of a licking than did perhaps any figure in the history of tele-mothering. She survived breast cancer and a subsequent mastectomy. She got through the trauma of her husband Jock's sudden death.

But of course, cancer and death are nothing compared to the ongoing guilt and shame associated with having brought a man named J.R. Ewing into the world. That's right: Miss Ellie (played with great presence by Barbara Bel Geddes) was the mother of dastardly, power-mad, and conniving J.R. (the incomparable Larry Hagman).

And as if that weren't awful enough, Ellie was also forced to endure the shooting death of another son, Bobby (Patrick Duffy), only to have that murder wiped from reality as Pamela Barnes Ewing's (Victoria Principal) elaborate hallucination. Yes, life got pretty weird for old Ellie. Her appearance was once radically altered when Bel Geddes left the show during the 1984–85 season and was replaced (in the same character) by Donna Reed. (Yes, that Donna Reed.)

Bel Geddes returned to the show the following season, however, and would remain with *Dallas* through 1990. Not that it allowed stability to return to Miss Ellie's life, of course. Her destiny was somehow always meant to be cloaked in misfortune and adversity. But oh, how that woman persevered. And my, how she stood behind those boys (even J.R., a man only a mother could love—and only barely).

Dallas, of course, was nothing short of a national phenomenon. Between 1979 and 1986, it finished in TV's ratings Top 10 every year—seven consecutive seasons in all (dropping to eleventh place in the eighth year). Moreover, from 1980 to '85, *Dallas* was television's top-rated show for three seasons and second-highest for two others. It would run for thirteen seasons and single-handedly spawn a nighttime soap opera craze that resulted in the spinoffs *Knots Landing, Falcon Crest, Dynasty,* and others.

The show centered on the wealthy Ewing oil family of Texas and the dysfunctional glory that would become their legacy. Sitting on the matriarchal throne overseeing the fighting, the backstabbing, and the cruelty was Miss Ellie, wife of Ewing Oil's primary shareholder, Jock (Jim Davis, who died early on in the show, necessitating the killing off of his character).

Ellie's greatest triumph as a mother was her discreet ability to operate as a safety net for her three boys (J.R., favorite son Bobby, and Gary, played by Ted Shackelford) as they operated Ewing Oil. That devotion would be tested often, particularly with J.R. But without Miss Ellie, the Ewings would have splintered into a million pieces. With her, they... well, OK, they still kind of splintered. She ultimately showed her favoritism by turning the oil company over to Bobby. But hey, with a kid like J.R., and Gary having long ago flown the coop, the lady had little choice. With this family, the fact Miss Ellie was still able to think clearly was the larger miracle.

Classic Mom-ents

🜸 Miss Ellie, concerned about a lump in her breast, has it checked out with a doctor. Tests confirm it is a malignant tumor. But her greatest concern is making sure her kids don't wrack themselves with worry—and that her husband Jock doesn't abandon her, since he left his first wife Amanda because of her disease. Ellie undergoes a mastectomy to save her life.

🜸 Garrison Southworth, the brother whom Miss Ellie believed to have died many years before, shows up at Southfork Ranch out of the blue with a young woman in tow. Jock and son J.R. suspect that he has resurfaced to claim the ranch as his inheritance. Ellie is wholly conflicted.

🜸 The Ewings are shocked to learn that their beloved Southfork has been mortgaged by the bank. It is left to Miss Ellie to ensure the future of her kids J.R. (who is responsible for the situation), Bobby and Gary by releasing part of the ranch for drilling, going against her father's last wishes to do so.

♀ Miss Ellie is left heartsick and paralyzed with worry when Jock goes on trial for a murder he did not commit—stemming from the discovery of a human skeleton on the ranch. Their kids (even J.R.) are traumatized, inspiring Ellie's maternal spirit to kick in and provide the rock they all need to get past this.

♀ As J.R. pulls strings behind the scenes, Ellie and Jock are locked into a massive feud over a project that could wind up in the selling off of Ewing Oil. Miss Ellie threatens to divorce her husband. J.R.'s scheme is falling into place. But it would invariably fall apart with his parents' reconciliation. And with that, Ellie is left with no choice but to essentially disown her son.

♀ A barbecue meant to celebrate a happy homecoming for Jock following his trip to South America takes a tragic turn. A phone call for Miss Ellie shatters the serenity. She announces to a stunned J.R. that his father—and her husband—has just been killed. Life at Southfork would never be the same again for Ellie.

*"I may never forgive
you for this, J.R."
—Miss Ellie*

119

Elyse Keaton
(*Meredith Baxter-Birney*)

Family Ties
(Sept. 22, 1982 to Sept. 17, 1989), NBC

Family Ties was originally created by producer Gary David Goldberg as a star vehicle for the actress who would be Elyse, Meredith Baxter-Birney. That it quickly turned into Michael J. Fox's show was something neither Goldberg nor Baxter-Birney could anticipate, and it reportedly inspired some veiled rancor that remained mostly concealed only because Fox comported himself as such an unassuming gentleman.

That, as they say, would qualify as the back story.

In the larger picture, Baxter-Birney's portrayal of Elyse Keaton was as distinctive as

any telemom depiction in the 1980s. Elyse was funky, she was sassy, she was different: a 1960s flower child and radical all grown up with professional responsibilities and three (later four) distinctively different kids. She also had a husband, Steven (Michael Gross), a onetime hippie himself who now managed a public television station.

What Elyse Keaton pioneered was the notion that a TV mom could be bright, involved, and opinioned and still allow her children the space, and the unequivocal acceptance, to be themselves. This was a fairly new concept back in 1982 when *Family Ties* premiered, ushering in the era of the generation-gap comedy (perfectly timed to coincide with America's evolution in its values during the Reagan years).

Elyse stood tall as the caring, if tough-minded, mom to the right-leaning elder teen Alex (Fox), popular girl Mallory (Justine Bateman), and young Jennifer (Tina Yothers), who was still years short of adolescence and miles away from having a clue about life. She suffered mostly silently through Alex's William F. Buckley posters and conservative business ideology. And Elyse was disciplined enough to allow her daughters to make their own mistakes.

This was a woman who struggled might-

ily to retain the hippie values she embraced in her formative years. There was an honesty about Elyse that would be rare in any TV era. Sure, she had her slipups, but she never tried to hide the fact that it was a struggle for her to adjust to '80s conservatism without compromising that '60s liberal outlook. And she admitted as much to the kids. The revelation often drew a blank stare from her oblivious brood, but she kept right on trying to explain her mindset, anyway.

Husband Steven perhaps grappled with this value evolution even more than did Elyse. But they got by and they got along. And Elyse always seemed to be there for the kids, even after she embarked on a full-time career as an architect in Middle America (actually Columbus, Ohio). Here was a generally realistic mom raising some pretty interesting children, and it looked neither effortless nor contrived.

That *Family Ties* survived for seven highly-rated seasons was clearly due to its plum Thursday night time slot following *The Cosby Show* on NBC. But the show also had plenty of real spark. And in Elyse, it featured a telemom who defined family sitcom trends for the 1980s and beyond.

Classic Mom-ents

♀ Elyse gives birth to baby Andrew (Brian Bonsall) in a much anticipated episode. Alex dreams that there is now another Republican mouth to feed. Elyse rather hopes he turns out slightly more liberal. So far, however, he's perfect, not to mention politically undeclared.

♀ Jennifer—no longer the baby of the family—feels left out after the birth of young Andrew. Elyse takes it upon herself to console her daughter and provide real understanding in between mid-night feedings.

♀ When Mallory's young teen girlfriend learns she's pregnant, she turns to Elyse for advice. It is the right place to come, as Elyse still has her idealistic, non-judgmental 1960s values in place. Alex, however, would challenge them regularly.

♀ Proving she can dish it out with the best of them when she has to, Elyse socks one of Alex's teachers in the jaw after he insults her. Alex is naturally embarrassed, appalled, and horrified. But for Elyse, it was simply a matter of defending her turf.

♀ Elyse has a challenge on her hands when she steals the show at a mother-daughter modeling contest—and Mallory can't hide her own hurt feelings at being ignored. She works hard to turn it into a life lesson, explaining to her daughter that these contests are all subjective—indeed, like life itself.

♀ When Mallory and Jennifer begin to pull away emotionally from their mother amidst the full onset of adolescence, Elyse takes the girls on a weekend vacation in the hope it will bring them closer together. It does—but only briefly.

"I think Alex's politics must come from your side of the family, Steven."
—Elyse Keaton

Clair Huxtable
(*Phylicia Rashad*)

The Cosby Show
(Sept. 20, 1984 to Sept. 17, 1992), NBC

Make no mistake: Clair Huxtable was, in virtually every area of life and behavior, perfect. Perfect wife. Perfect mother. Holder of a perfect white-collar professional job. Perfect balance struck between work and home. Perfect level of discipline instilled. Perfect temperament. She was sly, she was smart, she was fun, she was loving, she was steadfast, she was as solid as the Rock of Gibraltar.

And as if being the world's greatest mother and a damn fine legal aid lawyer

weren't enough, Clair was also African-African—meaning she was able to embrace such a healthy perspective and be so admirably together and successful while representing a racial minority.

Of course, that was really Clair's whole deal. The Huxtables didn't act like any black people we had ever seen before on TV. They were upscale, educated, cultured and classy in a TV comedy environment that had found pretty much all previous black families and characters cast as stereotypical, lowbrow loudmouths with at least three generations living under the same roof.

For this reason alone, *The Cosby Show* forever changed network TV. It also may have single-handedly saved the situation comedy, which had been careening toward extinction when Cosby arrived in 1984. It was the highest-rated comedy on TV in its first season (taking third overall behind *Dallas* and *Dynasty*). Then all the show did was finish first in the Nielsens for five consecutive seasons.

So whatever it was that Bill Cosby (obstetrician Cliff Huxtable) and Phylicia Rashad (dutiful wife and mother Clair) were dishing out, America had a ravenous appetite for it. Cosby, of course, was the linchpin in the whole deal. But Rashad was a surprisingly strong and appealing presence who oozed sass and self-confidence as the uncommonly wise Clair.

Clair surely was a supermom for the ages, a quick-witted woman who was able to bring up a brood of kids without the help of a nanny, work full-time and still keep her hubby feeling satisfied and supported. She represented the first upper-crust black professional mom to grace prime time, one who was able to juggle all of the pressurized elements of her life with flair.

Indeed, in Clair we had a mother with five kids who never appeared flustered and was able to approach every crisis with a level head. It helped that the children were shockingly mature and well-behaved. That Huxtable quintet was comprised of college-age daughter Sondra (Sabrina Le Beauf), overconfident teens Denise (Lisa Bonet) and Theo (Malcolm-Jamal Warner), eight-year-old dynamo Vanessa (Tempesst Bledsoe), and cute-as-a-button Rudy, age five (Keshia Knight Pulliam).

There were instances when all of the kids lied, did something unkind or dumb, or defied orders with back talk. But to Clair's credit (or perhaps good fortune), they never screwed up on a grand, or even minor, scale. Clair simply exuded the kind of firm authority that prevented the mischief from being carried to the next level.

It was uncanny. Even when Clair was throwing her weight around in court, the kids sensed her presence at home. And they cooperated, because one doesn't mess around with perfection.

Classic Mom-ents

🧍 Clair Huxtable and husband Cliff insist on meeting with Rudy's teacher to find out why their daughter is refusing to play the violin. When it turns out that Rudy is suffering from problems outside the classroom, Clair takes over with a gentle hand to get to the crux of the matter, which turns out to be an insecurity issue. Rudy just doesn't think she's good enough to measure up to her siblings. Clair assures her that she is, and that she loves her.

♀ When Theo comes home later than expected from a cross-country meet, Clair summons the Huxtable "family court" in order to uncover the reason. It was customary for Clair to combine her skills as a legal aid attorney with her no-nonsense mom instincts. More often than not, the truth would come out. In this case, it worked.

♀ Fed up with never having any alone time in her own home, Clair takes custody of a previously empty room and declares that it is now off-limits to everyone—whether she happens to be in it or not. The kids don't take their mother seriously, and they quickly live to regret it when mom catches them playing in the room. She takes it as a direct challenge to her authority. Groundings commence.

♀ While on a fishing trip, Theo accidentally catches a corpse. The ensuing media attention opens the lives of the Huxtables to unwanted public attention. Cliff is relatively accepting of it. So is Clair, until the glare of the spotlight begins to affect Theo's behavior. Uh oh. There will be no attitudes in Clair's household.

♀ Daughter Vanessa tells a lie so that she can spend time outside of the house with her boyfriend. When Clair catches wind of it, she keeps her cool but makes sure the seriousness of this kind of deception is understood and will not be tolerated. When Vanessa makes her case that she is on too short a leash, Clair assures her that as long as she lives under her roof, the leash size is her call.

♀ Eldest daughter Sondra gives birth to twins, which comes as a delightful shock to Clair, Bill, and the father's parents. It doesn't take long before the Huxtables are plotting ways to arrange babysitting duty. They drop by their daughter's house unannounced and make nuisances of themselves. Clair finally realizes that she and Bill have overstepped their bounds, and she sits her husband down to make sure he understands.

"Oh, I really don't think you want to know what I think, Theo."
—Clair Huxtable

Sophia Petrillo
(Estelle Getty)

The Golden Girls
(Sept. 14, 1985 to Sept. 12, 1992), NBC

After a certain age, many senior citizens seem to stop censoring themselves. They just blurt out whatever they please, age having eroded their self-control mechanism. This concept was the model used to create Sophia Petrillo (Estelle Getty), the scrappy, wisecracking old woman who shared a Miami home with her outspoken divorced daughter Dorothy (Bea Arthur) and widows Rose (Betty White) and Blanche (Rue McClanahan).

Sophia was the role of a lifetime for Getty. It allowed the actress to uncork most of the great lines on a series that would fly high as a Saturday night mainstay for NBC over seven hit seasons. Sophia was forced to move with her daughter and the other pair of oldsters on *The Golden Girls* after her retirement home burned to the ground. It would be a decision all lived to regret.

The biggest problem for anyone in her

midst was that Sophia appeared utterly incapable of controlling her sarcasm. No one

in the house could ask Sophia a simple question without receiving a mocking retort of some kind. If someone inquired whether she was wearing a revealing outfit, Sophia would snap, "No, I'm giving the leftover meatloaf a thrill. Why do you think it's hot as hell in here?"

Sophia had plenty of opportunity to exercise her acerbic muscles in the golden girl home. While Dorothy was more or less able to take her mother's comic venom in stride, it was tougher for Rose—a flaky, naive sort who misinterpreted almost everything— and Blanche, a lusty Southern belle who chased and caught men in her spare time (which was pretty much unlimited). Yet even when offended, the ladies dared not toss it back at Sophia. She would eat them for lunch, and dinner, too.

There were times when Sophia could be loving for brief periods. While competitive with her daughter, she would occasionally offer encouragement, support, a less-sarcastic-then-usual observation. But it was more in Sophia's nature to attack life, and motherhood, with a salty tongue. It made her days with those insufferable roomies pass infinitely quicker.

If Sophia was essentially a walking wisecrack, she was one accompanied by her own built-in sight gag. No old lady who looked as short and harmless as Sophia ever uttered the kinds of sharp daggers she fired on a regular basis. In her own odd way, the woman proved something of a revolutionary figure in telemothering: communicating a certain hope to elderly *Golden Girls* viewers that one can be gray, stooped and wrinkled and yet remain sharp as a tack.

Classic Mom-ents

♀ As a way of staying close to her daughter Dorothy, Sophia invades every potential private moment Dorothy has with her new boyfriend Raymond. Yet she doesn't feel a single ounce of guilt, having given up guilt in her fifties.

♀ When Dorothy's Uncle Angelo, a Sicilian priest, pays a visit to Florida, Sophia takes it as a personal challenge to keep her brother from discovering that Dorothy and Stan (Herb Edelman) are divorced. This is good, since he is planning the visit to coincide with what he believes to be the couple's fortieth wedding anniversary.

♀ Sophia is irate when Dorothy invites Sophia's feisty sister Angela to stay with them until she can find a place of her own in Miami—and then accuses Angela of trying to steal her man. There are, after all, only so many living men to go around in her age group.

♀ Motherly love is decidedly absent when Sophia joins forces with Rose to challenge Dorothy and Blanche in a bowling tournament. The bet: if Sophia's team wins, Dorothy must lend her airfare for a trip to Sicily with an old flame.

♀ When Stan tries to persuade Dorothy and Sophia to loan him money by taking them to a ball game, Sophia is hit in the head with a foul ball. Stan sees visions of big insurance bucks. But Sophia would hate to line Stan's pockets, the ball having knocked some rare sense into her.

"I was sleeping so well, I thought I'd try it in the sink."
—Sophia Petrillo

Nancy Weston
(Patricia Wettig)

thirtysomething
(Sept. 29, 1987 to Sept. 3, 1991), ABC

Yes, Nancy Weston was a self-absorbed yuppie. On *thirtysomething*, they all were. And yet, for her dysfunction, overanalysis, and insecurities, Nance was one very memorable TV mother. She always put her little kids Ethan and Brittany first, whether she was battling cancer or merely her own demons. It was personal sacrifice on a grand scale, the kind only a mother would make unquestioningly.

You might recall *thirtysomething* as that indulgent but extremely well-written and produced drama of the late 1980s that cast a

group of thirty-ish adult friends as the center of their own universe. There were crises galore, sometimes stimulated by the fact that the characters weren't feeling quite enough angst and feared something was therefore dreadfully wrong. But most of the time, their worst fears were reassuringly confirmed.

Take the case of Nancy (the captivating Patricia Wettig). The show wasn't three weeks old before she and Elliott (Timothy Busfield)—Nancy's eccentric man-child of a husband who was partnered in an ad agency with best friend Michael Steadman (Ken Olin)—were in the midst of serious marital strife and making plans to separate (which they soon did).

It was Nancy who had to nurture and reassure the couple's two school-age kids that everything would be OK. Her little son Ethan saw right through it and tumbled into an emotional free fall. While this was in progress, Nancy began writing a children's book about the anguish of a splintered home. It was therapeutic. But just as her tattered self-esteem was poised to receive a boost from the book's publication, she was diagnosed with cancer.

This was all a far cry from Nancy's idealistic expectations as a 1960s flower child and hippie who dressed in Indian-print skirts and spouted tribal wisdom. Now, after marrying young and bearing two kids while still something of a kid herself, it had come to this. Nancy did not handle it with the characteristic stiff upper lip. She whined. And she pouted. And she cried. And she sank into a hopeless funk.

Yet to her everlasting credit, Nancy mostly held it together for her beloved tykes. She was the only mother they had, and while that may not have been much sometimes, she understood that on some level she had to practice selflessness in at least one area of her life. Bravo.

As it happened, Nancy was pretty much the only semi-mature one in her circle of pampered Prozac-poppers. All busied themselves mourning their lost youth and struggling to find meaning in lives buttressed by $75,000 annual salaries and good health. They included Michael and annoying wife Hope Steadman (Mel Harris), the man-hunting Melissa (Melanie Mayron), fast-track head case Ellyn (Polly Draper), and shaggy-haired babe magnet Gary (Peter Horton).

By the time *thirtysomething* wrapped, Nancy had logged significant time mothering them all. And nobody did it better—or with a keener sense of melodrama.

Classic Mom-ents

Nancy Weston and husband Elliott are having serious marital problems that are complicated by the presence of two school-age children, Ethan (Luke Rossi) and Brittany (Jordana "Bink" Shapiro). When Elliott moves in temporarily with his business partner Michael Steadman and Michael's wife Hope and daughter Janey, Nancy is perplexed as to how to deal with Ethan's devastation and accompanying nightmares.

Nancy is tentative and unnerved when she goes on her first date since separating from Elliott. She doesn't quite know how to act and finally cuts the evening short, wondering why she had placed herself in a first-date position to begin with. Nancy freaks when she envisions how her kids would react to seeing her in a romantic situation with a man other than their father. She decides she isn't prepared to deal with that issue just yet.

Just as Nancy and Elliott are beginning to make a concerted effort to reconcile their marriage and have settled into a comfortable groove, Nancy's mother comes to visit and squelches their hard-earned marital progress. It makes Nancy re-evaluate her own behavior as a mother.

Ethan begins acting out in an especially severe way with his father's move back into the house and a recent rash of neighborhood robberies. Nancy makes extra time with her son to help quell his fears. But her sensitivity to his feelings proves insufficient for a boy who believes his security is at risk. It leaves Nancy feeling especially helpless.

Nancy discovers she has cancer and undergoes surgery immediately to remove the growth. As she recovers, the distance between her and Elliott only increases, and the side effects of chemotherapy impact her relationship with her kids. The feelings of despair serve to set bach Nancy's recovery.

"Oh no, it's the door! He's not supposed to be here until, like, 7:30! It's probably a Jehovah's Witness. Maybe they have something I can wear."
—Nancy Weston

Peg Bundy *(Katey Sagal)*

Married . . . With Children
(April 5, 1987 to July 7, 1997), Fox

When it comes to the mothers of television, the viewing audience has needed to learn to take the bad with the good—or even the wretched with the satisfactory. In the case of one Peg Bundy, however, an entirely different scale gauging competence and devotion was created to measure her status as a slothful loser without peer.

Simply put, there has never been a character in the annals of telemothering who even comes close to Peg at the bottom of the barrel. She is so far and away the worst TV mom of all time that it causes actual physical pain to analyze her woeful legacy. And yet...Peg Bundy belongs on any list of the tube's motherly memorables. No matter how one feels about her, the woman made a massive impact on American popular culture, a consequence from which the nation is still toiling to recover.

Peg (portrayed with uncouth glee by the talented Katey Sagal) was as much a cartoon character as were Wilma Flintstone and Jane Jetson. She was a colossal joke in an oversized wig and skyscraper pumps. *Married . . . With Children* itself was meant as a painfully lowbrow parody of the family sitcom—the anti-*Cosby Show*. It was raunchy in a hip, absurdly biting way.

While on some level we were supposed to believe that the Bundy family loved one another, they never really let it slip, covering any affection with disparaging, spiteful, and grossly insensitive responses.

There was Al (the inspired Ed O'Neill), a shallow and chauvinistic shoe salesman who lived to fire cruel verbal daggers at his wife. There was Peg, the laziest housewife on Earth. She neither cooked nor cleaned nor took care of her husband's sexual needs (if he even had any). Their primary form of communication was the unfeeling put-down. They argued about sex, money, and about how worthless the kids were. And all of it was discussed in front of those same kids.

The kids included a teenage blonde sexpot named Kelly (Christina Applegate) whose IQ seemed to plummet into the single digits. She followed mom and dad's lead by sparring mercilessly with her ne'er-do-well brother Bud (David Faustino), an eleven-year-old (when the show started) who appeared destined to be a bum like dear old dad.

That *Married . . . With Children* survived for ten and a half seasons was a sore point with many who objected to what they perceived to be the sitcom's galling indecency, a product of confusing satire with literalism. And as the show slashed and burned comic conventions during its decade of life, Peg carved out a niche as a housewife who didn't wife and a mother who didn't mother.

It was the ultimate example of TV's maternal icons coming full circle. With the pathetic Peggy, primetime had evolved from an image in which mothers could do no wrong to at least one mother who could do no right. It was clearly the dawn of a bold new anti-mom era.

Classic Mom-ents

Peg and husband Al insist on taking the kids on vacation to a cut-rate motel in

135

low-class Dumpwater, Florida, where an ax murderer who loathes tourists shows up every five years—and the locals bet he will strike again soon. During the Bundy stay, Peg ruins the family's fun by getting kidnapped by the axman, forcing Al to come to her rescue. It emerges that even as their mother is in peril, son Bud and daughter Kelly are callously calculating her odds of survival.

🚹 While Al teaches responsibility and the meaning of the dollar bill to Bud, Peggy tries to follow suit with a group of disinterested attendees during a mother-daughter career day at Kelly's school. Peg is stumped as to why no one will take her seriously, unaware that her materialism and sleazy appearance have undermined her efforts—and embarrassed Kelly.

🚺 In an effort to get elected queen at her high school reunion, Peg hands out bribes to the tune of $2,800. But an old archrival undercuts Peg with a bribery scheme of her own. Al's intervention is required to win his wife the crown. Meanwhile, Bud and Kelly crash the party to devour some real food. The moral of the story is: being a queen is much more important than feeding one's kids.

♀ Peggy purchases a computer to help her underachieving, slacker children with their schoolwork. But Al is disappointed that the machine won't bring him his slippers and dismisses it as a useless heap of junk. The computer ultimately gets more use as a hat rack than as a study tool.

♀ Because she flunked home economics, Peg discovers to her horror that she never really graduated from high school. She is thus required to go back and pass the class's final exam, embarrassing and humiliating Kelly worse than anything ever has in the girl's entire life.

"So . . . you really believe a nineteen-year-old in Playboy pouring honey on her tush is really interested in saving the environment?"
—Peg Bundy

Norma Arnold (Alley Mills)

The Wonder Years
(March 15, 1988 to Sept. 1, 1993), ABC

The Wonder Years was one of those rare shows that somehow transcended the bounds of TV and felt truly magical. Neither comedy nor drama but a poignant blend of both, it was a nostalgic throwback to suburban America in the late 1960s and the revolutionary changes the era wrought.

In the program's seriocomic milieu, we experienced society's growing tumult and evolving social mores through the eyes of a twelve-year-old innocent named Kevin Arnold (Fred Savage), whose narrative voice was that of the grown-up Kevin looking back at what he was feeling, and why it mattered (Daniel Stern supplied the voice-over). Kevin lived in the burbs with his parents, his brother, and a sister who was often away at college.

With the *Wonder Years* focus falling so overwhelmingly onto Kevin, it might seem that his mother would have been reduced to a forgettable appendage. But that was hardly the case with Norma Arnold (played by the extraordinary Alley Mills). It happens that by the time the series left the air five and a half years after it was launched, Norma had become one of the most quietly memorable figures in the annals of telemothering.

Yes, Norma was a supporting player in every sense of the term. She never said much, but she didn't need to. Her expressive eyes conveyed the frustration, pain, angst, despair, and denial of a woman who never seemed completely comfortable in her own skin. She didn't ask for contentment, figuring it just wasn't in the cards for her.

And so Norma crawled inside a domestic shell and survived. She was a housewife who used her mop and her spatula to keep life from getting too close. That extended to her often superficial relationship with Kevin, with Kevin's bullying and insensitive older brother Wayne (Jason Hervey), with her self-absorbed hippie daughter Karen (Olivia D'Abo), and even with her distant and domineering husband Jack (Dan Lauria).

We always sensed that Norma pined for more, longed to have an elaborate social circle and a greater grasp of the outside world, prayed for the inner capacity to let down her hair once in a while and not constantly worry about how she was going to buy the kids new socks on her limited budget. She wanted to have a happy life, but—somewhat tragically—she knew that was asking for too much.

Yet if Norma was not the warmest and savviest TV mom on the planet, she was notable for her sacrifices and her stability. No one could switch gears to remove herself from a troubling situation or conversation like she could. If we looked really closely, we saw just how much Norma loved those kids—which was, as it turned out, more than she loved herself.

In the age before enlightenment, it was just the way a good mom behaved.

Classic Mom-ents

♀ When Norma discovers a blood stain on her son Kevin's shirt after he returns from playing pick-up tackle football with his friends, she overreacts by following and spying on him constantly. Kevin is humiliated in front of his friends due to his mother's overprotective diligence.

♀ After her husband Jack stresses over income tax preparation and jumps on Norma for failing to find several receipts, she drives to church by herself, lights a candle, and says a prayer. Kevin follows his mother into the church, concerned that the taxes are putting a strain on their marriage. Instead it turns out her angst is due to her worry over the safety of the imperiled Apollo 13 astronauts. Norma is touched that Kevin cares about her feelings so much, lead-ing to a rare, stirring moment of bonding between the two.

♀ Kevin's nerdy friend Paul (Josh Saviano) is chosen, unofficially, as the brainiest kid in his class at school—bruising his ego, since brainy means "not cool." Norma comes to Paul's rescue, assuring him that "glasses make the man" and spending time with him to boost his spirits.

♀ After Norma takes a part-time job at Kevin's school, he finds that his mother's job sends his hipness quotient plummeting. Norma yells "Yoo-hoo!" to Kevin across the parking lot and in the hall, causing classmates to laugh and poke fun. But when his mom is fired for rampant forgetfulness, Kevin's embarrassment is replaced with compassion as he resolutely pulls his mother from an emotional hole.

♀ Norma is thrilled when her old stove breaks down, since it allows her to buy a new one with a "Meal-Finder" feature. But the fact that the family is short on money forces Jack to work longer hours. He even has to miss Thanksgiving, leaving Norma feeling particularly melancholy.

"Your father's had a bad day at work, so . . . no noise!"
—Norma Arnold

~4~
The 1990s
Nurture This!

As the 1990s blew in, a new icon of TV motherhood was just starting to get warmed up. Her name was Roseanne Conner (creation of Roseanne Barr/Arnold/Just Plain Roseanne), and she was everything that Mrs. Cleaver and Mrs. Brady were not: jowly, shrill, tart-tongued, domineering...and employed in a relatively menial job. She was also reluctant to try to solve every problem with a hug and a kind word. Her style was more a put-down and a handful of Chee-tos.

And yet *Roseanne* and her namesake maternal figure came to embody an edgier, more raw and anything-goes style of telemothering that typified the 1990s. *Roseanne* dragged the gritty, wart-filled side of life into the spotlight and simultaneously claimed a powerful, downright feminist voice for the matriarchs of the tube. With *Roseanne's* runaway success, the supermom officially died; the does-what-she-can-to-survive mom was now front and center. It no doubt gave us a clearer understanding of maternal realities than the primetime princesses of yore ever could manage to do.

There remained in the 1990s the occasional Pleasantville-style throwback to yesteryear's TV mom, in particular the steadfast doctor's wife Katherine Howser (Belinda Montgomery) of *Doogie Howser, M.D.* and the 1950s-emulating WB drama *7th Heaven*, where ma Annie Camden (Catherine Hicks) is a nonworking housewife whose five eldest kids (not including her twin babies) actually seem to respect both their parents and one another.

But during the final ten years of the century, those were significant exceptions to what came to be the motherly rule—that the old rules were, finally, dead and mostly buried. Even reasonable, patient, rock-solid Marge Simpson (voiced by Julie Kavner) of *The Simpsons* has had more going on inside that beehive-encrusted head of hers than many ever suspected.

The primary hallmark of telemotherhood throughout the '90s was the mom's tendency to dance (and rant) to the beat of her own drummer. This mother was a multi-faceted personality, doing her best to fulfill her domestic chores but not content to merely diaper and pack lunches and nurture their children's brains out. They longed for something more, though not necessarily to have it all. Few were ever shy about pointing out that they had feelings, they had libidos—and darn it, they had choices, too!

The decade's breed of TV mom rarely took any guff from anyone—not even from the vice president of the United States. Witness the reaction to Murphy Brown's (Candice Bergen) decision to remain single for the birth of her son in May 1992. Real-life Vice President Dan Quayle himself denounced Murphy as an example of the deterioration of family values in America.

Perhaps we shouldn't even ask why a vice president would feel compelled to become embroiled in the plotline of a TV comedy. Indeed, Murphy herself appeared unimpressed by the hubbub, chiding the

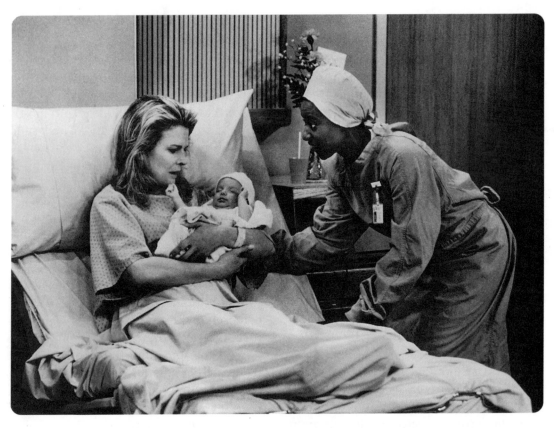

veep during a *Murphy Brown* episode the following season for his misspelling of the word "potato."

Hell hath no fury greater than a TV mother scorned.

We loved Murphy even as she struggled with the juggling act of career and parent. And she had company in moms like Grace Kelly (the one portrayed by Brett Butler in the comedy *Grace Under Fire*), a blue-collar woman who loved her three kids but went without a permanent mate rather than continue to settle for someone like her boozing ex-husband.

Then again, America in the 1990s embraced mommy role models who wound up being even more eccentric than Murphy and Grace. Take the mother of Eric Cartman on the crude Comedy Central cartoon *South Park*. She carried herself like a wholesome innocent while cooking up saturated fat-laced goodies for her grossly overweight son. Then we would find out the dark secret: she once graced the cover of a magazine serving the community of crack-addicted prostitutes. Oh yes, she was also a hermaphrodite.

Oh, the humanity....

Meanwhile, back on planet Earth, even the relatively traditional mother figures like *Home Improvement's* Jill Taylor (Patricia Richardson) and Texas-bred Peggy Hill (voiced by Kathy Najimy) of the Fox animated comedy *King of the Hill* carry the torch for a more feisty and outspoken version of the homebody. Both Jill and Peggy kept their sometimes overzealous husbands from self-destructing—particularly Jill, who was not only a vigilant, doting mom but a respected soulmate for husband Tim (Tim Allen). Their decisions were joint ones, resulting in mommy and daddy always presenting a united front.

Such telemotherly insight and confidence proved to be a rare bird during the 1990s, for this was also the decade that gave us such peerless TV mom busybodies as Marie Barone (Doris Roberts) of *Everybody Loves Raymond* and the ultra-neurotic Estelle Costanza (Estelle Harris) of *Seinfeld*. Marie, mother of Raymond (Ray Romano), believed that moms should be able to drop in on their sons (even married ones with kids) at all hours. Estelle, who brought George (Jason Alexander) into the world, was so boundary-challenged that she likely ruined her son's adult life before it ever began.

Of course, George could probably have had it even worse. He might have been raised by Livia Soprano (Nancy Marchand) and left to look over his shoulder for a hitman his mother might have hired (as she did unsuccessfully when looking to bump off her son Tony on HBO's *The Sopranos*).

What does it mean when the moms of primetime are reduced to trying to rub out their offspring? Does that represent a progression in the portrayal of motherhood? A regression? It wasn't terribly easy to tell one way or the other. But there was no denying that TV moms had become more eccentric, more colorful, more diverse and indeed more intriguing as a group than ever before.

As the millennium drew to a close and another half-century of TV mothering was launched, it was clear that moms had covered a large range of character territory in a scant fifty years of television life. The viewing audience is surely the richer for it.

Roseanne Conner
(Roseanne Barr/Arnold/Just Plain Roseanne)

Roseanne
(Oct. 18, 1988 to Aug. 26, 1997), ABC

Roseanne Barr's (as she was then known) arrival on the primetime scene heralded an overnight evolution and revolution that permanently transformed our notions about telemothering and its limits. She descended upon America's living rooms with all the subtlety of a drunken brawl, challenging viewers to accept a mother who ate Chee-tos by the bag, weighed too much, wore the pants in the family, and struggled to keep even a menial job—and didn't always like her kids.

ABC didn't really know what it was getting when it plucked Roseanne from the stand-up comedy circuit. She was a Denver housewife (or "Domestic Goddess" as she called it), and her routine was inspired by her life of kids and soccer games, and living with a husband who drank beer and fell asleep in an overstuffed chair in front of the TV set.

Roseanne hit the air in 1988 as the pied piper of maternal angst. Her namesake show struck an immediate nerve, slashing and burning all of the old TV mom notions about subservience and apron strings and tidy little issues. It also was blessed with a talented supporting cast that included John Goodman as Roseanne's equally portly husband Dan Conner, Laurie Metcalf as sister Jackie, and Lecy Goranson, Sara Gilbert, and Michael Fishman as kids Becky, Darlene, and David (or D.J.), respectively. Estelle Parsons, Martin Mull, Ned Beatty, and Sandra Bernhard—among others—would join later.

Roseanne did nothing less than change TV comedy over its nine seasons and was, along with *Home Improvement,* the most popular sitcom of the 1990s. But it was more than that. The show's great success signified the death knell for the contrived situations of the 1950s and '60s family series, confirming that the audience was ready to accept—and even embrace—imperfection in the motherly heroines of tube history. It also signaled the desire to see a less sugar-coated version of familial reality.

In some ways, *Roseanne* was a descendant of blue-collar family comedies like *The Honeymooners* and *All in the Family*. There was but one key difference: in the Conner household, the mom ran the show. And the husband more or less accepted it.

During the course of its run, *Roseanne* would deal with pretty much every issue and crisis that might be faced by spouses and children, aside from divorce. And mom Roseanne was unconcerned about how her bitter sarcasm and tart tongue impacted the kids. When one would ask, "Mom, why are you so mean?", she might reply in jest, "Because I hate kids...and I'm not your real mom." There were also threats of mom selling the children on the black market. Not exactly the snuggly security blanket of yore.

Yet there was never a question that Roseanne loved her kids in a wholly unconditional way, which would come in handy when they turned out to be dysfunctional teenagers and adults. Becky ran off and eloped before she was eighteen. Tomboy Darlene and her boyfriend split and reunited every forty-eight hours or so. D.J. also had his screw-ups. The truths in life were all right there on screen, as were recurring gay characters including those played by Mull and Bernhard.

Behind the scenes, meanwhile, Roseanne would marry and then suffer a bitter breakup with series writer and co-star Tom Arnold. The atmosphere on the set was often said to be combative and difficult. But what aired week after week was more often than not superb. And Roseanne, flaws and all, made TV mom history by flaunting her abundant imperfections.

Classic Mom-ents

♀ Roseanne is crestfallen when her daughter Darlene has an appendicitis attack and must undergo an emergency appendectomy just hours after Roseanne had yelled at the girl a bit too forcefully. Irrationally, Roseanne feels somehow responsible for Darlene's hospitalization, and vows to be less critical and explosive with her in the future. Temporarily, a tighter bond between mother and daughter results.

♀ When the time seems right, Roseanne decides to have "the talk" with daughter Becky about sex and pregnancy and protection. What she doesn't know is that it's her younger daughter Darlene who could better use the advice, since Darlene is close to becoming sexually active. It comes as a minor shock to Roseanne, who suddenly isn't quite as comfortable giving the birds and bees speech. But she tries to, anyway.

♀ The stuff hits the fan when Roseanne and hubby Dan decide to enforce a curfew on the girls. Their strategy is received less than enthusiastically by Becky and Darlene, who pretty much ignore the rule. Roseanne takes this as an insult and agrees with Dan to suspend their social privileges until proper respect for house regulations can be shown.

♀ Becky tells her mother that it might indeed be a good idea for her to go on the pill, given her increasingly physical relationship with her boyfriend. Roseanne freaks, but quietly. She is supportive of her daughter's responsible approach to birth control yet a bit dazed by the fact Becky is already sexually active. Roseanne ultimately realizes that her discomfort is more about her issue than Becky.

♀ Roseanne accuses son D.J. of bringing marijuana into the house. Then Dan comes clean with the truth, and it has nothing to do with D.J. The stash Roseanne found belonged instead to her husband. She isn't sure how to react to the news but figures that, at the very least, D.J. deserves an explanation. He gets it.

♀ When she is surprised to find herself pregnant, Roseanne considers having an abortion. But no matter what she opts to do, she is adamant that this be her decision—and hers alone. She chooses to keep the baby, which throws the Conner household into a blizzard of conflicting emotions.

"Now I know why some animals eat their young."
—Roseanne

149

Murphy Brown
(Candice Bergen)

Murphy Brown
(Nov. 14, 1988 to Aug. 10, 1998), CBS

Anyone who wasn't living inside a climate-controlled, subterranean geodesic dome will recall the furor in May 1992 that swirled around the birth of a baby boy to neurotic Murphy Brown (Candice Bergen) on *Murphy Brown.* Murph's rejection of marriage proposals from both potential fathers set off a firestorm of controversy that extended clear to the White House.

Vice President Dan Quayle himself weighed in on the issue of Murphy's fatherless birth during a speech in San Francisco in which he cited the show as an example of the deterioration of family values in America. He charged that Murphy Brown was "mocking the importance of fathers" by having Murphy "bearing a child alone and calling it just another lifestyle choice."

Well! The republic quickly came unraveled over that one. *Murphy*'s creator-producer Diane English shot back, "If he believes that a woman cannot adequately raise a child without a father, then he'd better make sure abortion remains safe and legal." Yikes! Talk about a can of worms.

Of course, the incensed posturing and indignant retorts from the *Murphy* brass concealed the fact they were all quietly overjoyed. Quayle could not possibly have supplied the series with a greater ratings boost than his speech that set off a national controversy. *Murphy Brown* benefited greatly from this ratings shot in the arm, and used it to unfurl story lines that mocked Quayle unmercifully.

What was nearly forgotten in the furor was that Murphy was now indeed a mother, if a partnerless one. She doted on little boy Avery Brown (played at various points between 1994 and '98 by Dyllan Christopher, Jackson Buckley, and Haley Joel Osment, who has since gone on to great fame with *The Sixth Sense*).

And what kind of a TV mom was Murphy? Well, she turned out to be a predictably conflicted one, caught between the tug-and-pull of career and parenthood. Her job as the driven superstar reporter for the TV magazine *F.Y.I.* required Murph to find a full-time nanny, a search that proved amusingly fruitless until her off-kilter painter pal Eldin (Robert Pastorelli) stepped forward to fill the nanny gap.

However, as the months and years crept

by, Murphy gradually tapped into her own family values. She scaled back on her office duties and travel to spend more time with the boy she doted on. Of course, this being Murphy, Avery was often thrust into the parental role to keep his mom on track. That was especially true when Murphy came down with breast cancer—and Avery became her rock.

It was ultimately quite ironic that once the countercharges and chest-thumping died down, Murphy showed that she could raise a perceptive and well-adjusted kid without a conventional daddy figure. She was as nuts as ever, but Murphy finally was able to tap into a tender and nurturing side that transformed her from a self-absorbed workaholic into a memorable TV mom. It's the kind of evolution that not even a finger-wagging vice president can denigrate.

Classic Mom-ents

After her plane from New York back home to Washington is delayed by fog, Murphy stresses over the fact she will have to miss Avery's first birthday party. She tries everything to get back—to no avail. A crestfallen Murphy decides she can't do it all and plans to give her priorities an overhaul.

Murphy brazenly trades on her contacts and notoriety to get Avery accepted into the prestigious Ducky Lucky Preschool, inviting the facility's board members to a party bursting with celebrities. The woman clearly will stop at nothing for this boy.

The shameless Murphy takes Avery to a White House Easter egg hunt as a way of improving her chances for an interview with the president. Instead, her infant son makes such a fuss that it results in Murphy's permanent banishment from the White House. It would be the last time Murphy tried to use her son to better her job standing.

Murphy worries about how she is going to tell little Avery about her trip to the hospital to treat an illness (cancer) that she can't bring herself to mention in the wake of her breast cancer diagnosis. But after meeting with a wise cancer survivor, Murphy is finally able to utter the word, freeing her emotionally to discuss it with the boy. He turns out to be far less traumatized than she.

For her own reasons, Murphy is consumed by the need to explain the concept of death to son Avery. So she sets out to glean the death perspectives of everyone in the *F.Y.I.* office where she works, and this distresses many of them. But her co-workers figure this is simply part of Murphy's healing process and agree to humor her—which leaves a few of them suddenly concerned for their own mortality.

"Well, I used to park the car in the closet, but I found it wrinkled my clothes."
—Murphy Brown

Libby Thatcher *(Patti LuPone)*
Life Goes On
(Sept. 12, 1989 to Aug. 29, 1993), ABC

It took until the 1990s before network TV would give us a mother who was challenged with raising a handicapped kid in a weekly series. The show was *Life Goes On*. The mother was Libby Thatcher (played by Broadway actress Patti LuPone). The kid was eighteen-year-old Charles "Corky" Thatcher (portrayed by Christopher Burke). And Corky's illness was Down syndrome.

But the show, while occasionally maudlin and grim, turned out to be quite admirable. For one, it had the courage to use an actor (Burke) who was actually afflicted with a mild form of Down. And within the story line, Corky wasn't carted off to special schools or babied, but mainstreamed in a regular high school (apparently after years of special education courses).

A fair share of the credit deserves to go to LuPone, the first TV mom ever to have won a Tony award—and for *Evita,* no less. LuPone even did a little bit of singing in the show as alter ego Libby considers pursuing the showbiz career she stopped when raising Corky became top priority. She was a working mother during *Life Goes On's* four seasons, but that work came mainly in a high-stress ad agency.

But one of the great things about Libby was her resilience and versatility. She could be happy doing the pressurized white-collar job, or helping sensitive husband Drew run the restaurant he ultimately opened, or even just playing housewife.

This afforded *Life Goes On* the opportunity to explore not only how a typical family treats a member with special needs but also the ways his affliction impacts the community at large. The drama still wound up being essentially a soap opera of coming-of-age angst, yearning, and trauma, but it also had an edge that made it somewhat nobler.

As she turned forty, Lib surely had plenty to keep her busy at the homestead. Daughter Becca (Kellie Martin) encountered a new crisis pretty much every day as a high school freshman who tried desperately to fit in with her peers—a tough thing when your brother sticks out like a sore thumb. There was of course Corky, struggling to find a little independence and dignity in a world that was reluctant to grant it. And often, Drew's screw-up of a daughter, Paige (Monique Lanier and later Tracey Needham), came to live with the Thatchers, carting along her own jumbo can of worms.

So it's clear enough that Libby didn't have it really easy. Her tough hide and uncanny ability to compartmentalize her life and emotions would come in handy. Even when the stress and the muck piled up in front of her like a mud slide, Libby remained a pillar of calm amid the various storms. She allowed Corky all of the space he wanted and needed, empathized with Becca through every adolescent hormonal shift, and still found time to lend focused and loving support to the needy Drew. Quite a mom, this Libby Thatcher.

Classic Mom-ents

♀ Daughter Becca gets a first-hand look at what life is like in her working mother's hectic corporate world when she videotapes a day in Libby's life at her advertising job. It would prove jarring for Becca to watch her mother navigate the choppy waters of her work environment. Lib isn't comfortable watching herself on-screen, either. The incident briefly divides Libby and her daughter before being forgotten.

♀ Libby and husband Drew find their dream vacation turn into a nightmare after son Corky wins a trip to Hawaii as a raffle prize. When the family gets there, the luggage is lost, the hotel is rundown and teeming with small reptiles, and their discount coupons have

expired. Libby has had enough within hours and makes plans to go home. Then entertainer Don Ho intercedes to diffuse the crisis, and Libby's kids catch a rare glimpse of what their mother looks like when the anxiety drains from her body and she lets down her hair.

♀ It mystifies Libby when she begins seeing nighttime visions of a young boy. Then she discovers she's pregnant and it starts to make some sense to her. Meanwhile, Libby must reassure Becca and Corky that having a new sibling will be OK—even if they weren't consulted first.

♀ The often overprotective Libby is skeptical when Drew's bubbly brother pays the Thatchers a visit. At about that time, Corky wonders aloud who will care for him after his parents are gone. Libby convinces her husband to entrust that responsibility to his contrite brother if they die first.

♀ Libby must play peacemaker and diplomat against her better instincts when her bickering parents come to visit. She feels caught between her re-ignited pain from childhood and her determination to protect her kids from being exposed to such a negative depiction of marital life.

"You can be anything you want to be, Corky. You just have to want it bad enough."
—Libby Thatcher

Harriette Winslow
(JoMarie Payton)

Family Matters
(Sept. 22, 1989 to July 17, 1998), ABC and CBS

Family Matters was in fact a spinoff from the one-time ABC hit comedy *Perfect Strangers*, which featured JoMarie Payton (then Jo-Marie Payton-France) as a busybody elevator operator named Harriette Winslow. Harriette would continue on in the new comedy as the sassy, take-no-jive wife of a heavyset cop named Carl (Reginald VelJohnson), and mother to teenagers Eddie (Darius McCrary) and Laura (Kellie Shanygne Williams) and prepubescent Judy (Jaimee Foxworth).

They shared a home in Chicago with Carl's irascible mom, Mother Winslow (Rosetta LeNoire), Harriette's widowed sister Rachel (Telma Hopkins), and Rachel's infant son Richie (identical twins Joseph and Julius Wright). And later, their happy home would be invaded by a loose-limbed nerd named Steve Urkel

(Jaleel White). That ultimately made Harriette seem like Urkel's mom, although in fact he was merely a neighbor who more or less adopted the Winslows.

It would quickly become a sore point with Payton-France that this was supposed to be her and VelJohnson's show, only to have it turn into a venue for the slapstick Urkel and his hiked-up pants, oversized glasses, and cloying whine of a voice. But a hit is a hit, and Payton-France was able to ride the *Family Matters* train for nine seasons—making it the longest-running black-themed TV series ever.

That Urkel would change the Winslows' lives from the moment White guest-starred in his first episode midway through the first season was never in question. But it didn't hold Harriette back from becoming a memorable telemom who was able to nurture even in the face of her own mother's hovering gaze.

In the Winslow household, Harriette was a reliant, supportive presence who had a more authoritative voice than her husband Carl. The brassy persona occasionally seemed stereotypical, but that was perhaps more due to Carl's being overwhelmed than Harriette's henpecking. She counseled her own kids with a reassuring concern and a gentle hand, and was always there when needed.

Now Urkel, on the other hand, was something else altogether. He was all over the map, a virtual human cartoon with a rubber body that appeared to be controlled by forces outside of his control. Harriette sometimes had to lay down the law to keep Urkel centered in this galaxy—but the woman never shrank from a confrontation or a difficult discussion, though she rarely sought them out, either. The bottom line was that Harriette had to be one strong mama. She survived Urkel and lived to tell the tale.

Classic Mom-ents

♀ When her daughter Laura violates her curfew, Harriette is forced to crash a party wearing her rollers and robe to pull the girl out. The embarrassed Laura and her infuriated mother then have it out over why it was necessary to make such a scene. Laura accuses Harriette of trying to humiliate her. Harriette explains to her daughter that she did all the humiliating on her own.

♀ Harriette approves of Laura going out on an unsupervised cheerleading event, but her wary husband Carl does not. Urkel soon checks in and casually mentions that a guy Laura likes is going to be at the event. But it's too late. Laura is already on her way. Urkel is dispensed to spy on the girl and finds her flirting like crazy. He reports it back to Harriette, who feels somewhat betrayed. Laura swears it was all innocent and vows to kill Urkel.

♀ Carl has a huge fight with son Eddie over his money-handling skills, and Eddie is so incensed that he decides on the spot to move out. Harriette attempts to intercede, speaking to both men about how passionate each is for his own point of view—and how that doesn't make either one of them wrong. The men disagree and begin arguing with Harriette instead. But Eddie decides not to move out after all.

♀ How has Steve Urkel destroyed the Winslows' lives? We see in flashback everything he has done to make Harriette and her husband and children ready for therapy. All agree the guy has driven them batty. But Harriette is left to remind them that Urkel has saved their hides on occasion, too.

♀ Urkel tries to warn Laura that her date is going to be a bunch of trouble, but naturally she doesn't listen. After hearing that the guy taunted Laura as "a baby" for not going further with him physically, Harriette sits her daughter down for a heart-to-heart and assures her she did the right thing.

"Carrrrrrllll!!!!!"
—Harriette Winslow

Marge Simpson
(*Julie Kavner*)

The Simpsons
(Dec. 17, 1989 to present), Fox

There is almost no disputing the fact that Marge Simpson (voiced by Julie Kavner) has earned a certain status as the most enduring and complex mother figure in the history of TV animation. She is the family peacemaker, the voice of reason, the steady, sturdy counterpoint to her agreeably slobby, beer-swilling husband Homer.

Marge is gentle. She's caring. She loves her kids Bart, Lisa, and Maggie for all she is worth. And she has that distinctive, towering blue beehive hairdo that is miraculously held together with a single bobby pin.

Marge cooks marshmallow squares that are said to be miraculous and is equally skilled at whipping together heaping plate-

fuls of unidentifiable, gelatinous purple gunk. She is warm. She is intelligent. She is loyal. She rarely complains. She is indeed the thread that holds the dysfunctional Simpson clan together.

And yet, there is surely far more to Marge Simpson than meets the eye. Consider that her skin is yellow, she has a horrendous overbite, and she possesses only four fingers on each hand. That's just for starters. She may be the ultimate homebody, but she was also once nearly lured into an affair with a slick French bowling instructor named Jacques who told her "Your fingers are so slender, so feminine…"

Not quite your typical low-key housewife, Marge has worked as a beat cop, served time in prison for shoplifting a bottle of bourbon, gone on the lam with a female car thief in unsettling *Thelma and Louise* style, and once became addicted to slot machines. Then there was the time that Marge led a community-wide protest against cartoon violence over the bloody *Itchy & Scratchy Show*. She even logged time as a strikebreaking teacher, a carhop waitress, a nuclear power plant worker, and an actress (in a production of the musical *Oh! Streetcar*.

However, in the cleverly subversive environment of *The Simpsons*, it is Marge who is the stable and earthbound one. She often goes without so her family is never deprived, but she rarely acts like a martyr. She is genuinely happy to sacrifice for those she loves—even Homer, whom she allows to be in charge despite his terminal buffoonery.

It's one of the well-hidden secrets of the show's long-term success that this is a com-edy about people who—deep down inside—love one another. And it is Marge who defines that bond.

Classic Mom-ents

In order to be a better parent to her kids following a near nervous breakdown, Marge decides to take a vacation alone at the Rancho Relaxo Resort. Marge lives it up, pampering herself with champagne and caviar, while son Bart and daughter Lisa struggle with their aunts Patty and Selma, and Homer is clueless in taking care of baby Maggie. Marge's stock as a mom skyrockets.

Marge takes Lisa for a complete makeover to help boost her confidence as an entrant in the Little Miss Springfield beauty pageant. Lisa would be voted runner-up but captures the crown when the winner is struck by lightning.

Marge, Homer, and the kids attend an "Inner Child" seminar in Springfield because Marge believes it will promote clearer family communication. Her original inspiration is a self-help videotape hosted by Troy McClure, whose past self-help videos include "Smoke Yourself Thin" and "Get Confident, Stupid." McClure makes Marge believe that the key to closer relationships is tapping one's inner child. Instead, her family members wind up accessing their inner rage.

When Lisa is struck with a bad case of the blues, Marge consoles her by saying, "Take all of your bad feelings and push them down, all the way down, past your knees, until you're almost walking on them. And then you'll fit in, and you'll be invited to parties, and boys will like you . . . and happiness will follow."

To teach son Bart a lesson, Marge gives him the cold shoulder after he is caught on a store security tape shoplifting an extremely violent video game. Bart fears he's lost his mother's love for good and returns to the store to purchase the game with real money. The lesson Bart learns is that love can be conditional.

"The only thing I'm high on is love. Love for my son and daughters. Yes, a little LSD is all I need."
—Marge Simpson

Jill Taylor
(Patricia Richardson)

Home Improvement
(Sept. 17, 1991 to May 25, 1999), ABC

It can be said with a reasonable degree of assurance that Jill Taylor is one of the top three or four toughest TV moms in the rich and eclectic history of telemothering. With all of that testosterone careening through her home, Jill had to be a gutsy gal merely to survive.

Think about it. Jill (the vivacious Patricia Richardson) had *Tool Time* host

Tim Taylor (comedian extraordinaire Tim Allen) and all of those drill bits and soldering irons to contend with. And then on top of that, she was saddled with three rambunctious young sons: Brad (Zachery Ty Bryan), Randy (Jonathan Taylor

Thomas), and Mark (Taran Noah Smith). The woman had to be a tower of patience and fortitude to persevere under these exceedingly male conditions.

And yet, Jill always gave at least as well as she got. The wisecracks flowed, often through a haze of frustration. Yet this stellar wife and mom also managed to be nurturing. And soft. And vulnerable. And sensitive. Indeed, Allen was fortunate to cast an actress as versatile and charismatic as Richardson turned out to be. She was the perfect wifely foil and an engaging, energetic, and understanding TV mom. It's a rare combination that Jill made look easy.

Home Improvement broke from the starting gate in 1991 and was an immediate smash hit for ABC. It was essentially an extension of Tim Allen's power-tool stand-up comedy persona. He was the sassy schmoe who was in love with the way fix-it tools felt in his hands—"More Power!" was his mantra—but had little idea of how to harness that power. The joke was that he hosted his own TV show and was known as The Tool Man.

Meanwhile, at home Tim was a devoted husband and father who lived to teach his sons the wonders of chainsaws and heavy-duty everything. Jill was endlessly vexed by her husband's tool-driven misadventures but rose above the fray by having a life of her own. She pursued a master's degree in psychology and did part-time counseling out of the house.

Yet while Jill clearly wasn't satisfied being a full-time stay-at-home mom, we always sensed that the family had to come first (even before her own satisfaction). And as the boys grew into little men, Jill always remained the rock-solid force who kept the Taylor household from crumbling into a pile of plywood.

Classic Mom-ents

♀ When Al (Richard Karn) approaches Tim to voice the possibility that one of his sons stole an expensive Swiss Army knife from the hardware store, his wife Jill refuses to believe her guys could lie and steal. Jill tries to talk Tim out of searching their room—calling it a trust issue. But Tim searches anyway—and the missing knife turns up in Mark's dirty laundry. Jill is very surprised and hurt, but a reassuring explanation soon emerges: an acquaintance of Mark's slipped the knife into his pocket without his knowledge.

♀ When Mark's teacher informs Jill and Tim that the boy is having trouble in school, Jill fears that the problem could be her own neglect. She wracks herself with guilt. But as it turns out, Mark's issue isn't mother-related. He simply needs glasses and is afraid he will look dumb and become the butt of jokes.

♀ Randy winds up in the hospital emergency room with a sprained arm after he's hurt in a sledding race. Jill's first instinct is to prevent him from doing any more sledding, since Randy could injure himself further. But when Jill finds out that he wants to race to counteract the fact that he is the shortest kid in his class, she backs off.

♀ When Jill's sister Carol finds out she is pregnant with a baby girl, Jill wistfully reflects on the fact she always wanted a daughter but had three boys instead. Randy and Brad hear this and tell young Mark that mom wishes he had been a girl, upsetting Mark greatly until Jill can set things straight.

♀ Jill is devastated and mortified to learn that she has uterine cancer, forcing an emergency hysterectomy. Problems arise during the surgery. She worries that her kids will have to grow up without a mommy. The operation proves a success, though Jill's ovaries have to be completely removed.

"So, you just got up and said, 'Oh, what a beautiful morning. I think I'll humiliate my wife today'?"
—Jill Taylor

Estelle Costanza (*Estelle Harris*)

Seinfeld

(Feb. 8, 1992 to Sept. 10, 1998), NBC

There has likely never been, and will never again be, a telemother as boldly, unforgivingly neurotic as was Estelle Costanza (Estelle Harris) of *Seinfeld*. On the ultimate "show about nothing," Estelle was a mother who always managed to make something out of nothing. And her poor son George (Jason Alexander) suffered the brunt of it. Whatever was left of Estelle's incessant anxiety was aimed at husband Frank (Jerry Stiller), who always seemed a little better equipped to handle it.

Anyone who wondered why George had turned out to be such an angst-riddled nebbish need look no further than Estelle. She surely made George what he was: self-centered, unreliable, immature, impulsive, lacking in self-worth. Indeed, she continued to rag on her son with the same regularity and intensity as when he was growing up. She believed her role in life was to keep George from imploding; instead, she helped make him a basket case.

But both Estelle and the actress who played her—Harris—had a certain spunk that made them loveable in spite of themselves. Estelle had that paranoid, whiny New York Jewish thing in spades. She saw glasses as half-empty and people as half-witted.

George? Estelle believed that her son comported himself with the specific intent of upsetting her. To Estelle, it was a slight that her son wasn't allowing her to run his life for him. Heck, she had already done it for forty years or so and what was so wrong?

Well…everything was wrong, of course. And that was both the problem and the fun of it. *Seinfeld*, you see, was an engine driven by neurosis. It was about five eccentric single people in Manhattan named George, Jerry (Jerry Seinfeld), Kramer (Michael Richards), Elaine (Julia Louis-Dreyfus), and Newman (Wayne Knight) who had yet to experience real life and responsibility. And in fact, they never really would.

For this quintet, the minutiae of life prevailed, whether it be obsessing over Pez dispensers and puffy pirate shirts or holding contests to see who could hold out the longest from relieving themselves sexually. They were children residing in adult bodies, which was one reason why Estelle felt so perfectly justified in making her son's life miserable. He deserved it because he was such a nobody. If he would only listen to her a little bit more…

It would never happen. In the end, Estelle couldn't even save George from prison. But this was one TV mom who never let reasonable boundaries stand between her and her peculiarly endearing brand of motherly love.

Classic Mom-ents

♀ Estelle accidentally interrupts her son George while he's in his room masturbating to an open copy of *Glamour* magazine. She immediately falls over and throws out her back, putting her in the hospital—all because of her son's...you know.

♀ When money gets a little tight for George, Estelle and her husband Frank agree to let him move back into their house. But Estelle lets her son know that they believe his new job as a hand model has inspired him to become unnaturally obsessed with keeping his hands safe. George now scarcely uses his hands for anything other than photographs. His mother finds this behavior sick. But like everything else in George's life, the hand-model gig would be short-lived.

♀ After George is arrested along with Elaine, Jerry and Kramer for failing to come to the aid of a man being robbed in upstate New York, Estelle attempts during their subsequent trial to bribe the judge to be lenient with her boy. It doesn't work, but it is endearing nonetheless.

♀ George takes his fiancée Susan's parents to meet his own parents for the first time, which results in Estelle leading a vocal protest over the fact that a loaf of rye bread was not served with the meal. She would not easily forgive the slight.

♀ Estelle punishes George for failing to keep their home tidy while he stayed there, grounding him for finding an unused condom and failing to unearth a missing copy of *TV Guide* (which George had given to Elaine). The condom was one thing; giving away *TV Guide* was a sin beyond repair.

"I walk into my son's room, and he's treating his body like it's an amusement park!"
—Estelle Constanza

Jamie Buchman
(Helen Hunt)

Mad About You
(Sept. 23, 1992 to Aug. 5, 1999), NBC

A baby named Mabel landed in the lives of married Manhattan professionals Jamie and Paul Buchman as the fifth season of the hit NBC sitcom *Mad About You* drew to a close. As played by Helen Hunt (who earned three Emmys for the role) and Paul Reiser, the addition of a screaming, whimpering, retching, diaper-soiling ball of needy flesh pretty much sent them sprinting off the deep end.

This turned out to be particularly true of Jamie, who was transformed overnight from mild head case to complete basket case by this blessed event. Indeed, it was as if thousands of years of

maternal know-how and understanding had been erased by a single yuppie birth. It somehow proved to be charming and pathetic simultaneously.

Jamie established a benchmark for tele-mom angst that is not likely to be equaled anytime soon. From the moment that Mabel left her womb, Jamie was transformed into an obsessive, reactive jumble of frayed nerves. Poking fun at a late 1900s creation—first-time parents who make a federal case of every sneeze and bodily secretion and act as if they are the first people to understand what an all-consuming job parenting really is—Jamie and Paul allowed the tyke to play Twister with both of their minds.

They stayed up all night comforting the kid, tried to plan her preschool before Mabel was eating strained carrots, and talked nonstop about every aspect of her physical life. Each burp was a revelation, every poopy diaper a miracle. Jamie was uncomfortably intense, and then came her postpartum: not a pretty thing at all. Yet it was oddly entertaining to see a mother who represented such a manic extreme.

By the final season of *Mad About You*, Jamie had settled down to become a decent little mommy and, if anything, spent too little time fussing and fawning over the baby. We might still view it as merciful, though, that the series didn't stay on long enough to see what Jamie would have been like with her little girl four or five years down the road. We can only guess at the potential therapy bills—for all three of them.

Even so, Jamie is due some thanks for sharing with us a first-time mama mindset we should all work like heck to avoid.

Classic Mom-ents

- Jamie and Paul's daughter Mabel is born, though at the time of the birth they had no idea what they were going to call this child. In fact, they had yet to come up with a name even as Jamie checked out of the hospital.

- Jamie's post-baby freak-out begins innocently enough: she writes a letter to her infant daughter to be read on her eighteenth birthday. But quickly, she moves on to scouting out top-of-the-line preschools for Mabel—who is at this point only two weeks old.

- A devastating postpartum depression consumes Jamie. It is the worst case of the motherly blues that anyone has ever witnessed. She is heard to be railing so savagely against marriage and parenthood in a beauty salon one day that a young woman within earshot calls off her own wedding.

- After five months without sexual contact following Mabel's delivery, Jamie seeks the counsel of a new neighbor—a divorced mother of three—who works to teach Jamie a more casual and less kamikaze style of parenting.

- Jamie and Paul comfort one another through the excruciatingly painful process of training Mabel to understand that they won't always rush to pick her up when she cries. She finally cries herself to sleep, but not before the couple has discussed every end of the issue at great length.

- Jamie and Paul decide to fly separate planes when they take their first trip without Mabel since her birth, operating on the theory that if one plane goes down, they don't want to leave her orphaned. Jamie winds up missing her baby so much that she instinctively starts mothering everyone on the plane.

"I'm having a clothing problem because suddenly, I'm shaped like a Dr. Seuss character."
—Jamie Buchman

170

Grace Kelly
(Brett Butler)

Grace Under Fire
(Sept. 29, 1993 to Feb. 17, 1998), ABC

Say this much for hard-nosed, divorced TV mom Grace Kelly: she had her priorities mostly in order. Her kids always came first, far ahead of the succession of male suitors who existed to make her life miserable. Leading that list was Grace's ex-husband, Jimmy.

On the other hand, everybody on *Grace Under Fire* either had an ex or was an ex. The producers should have just gone and called this show *The Ex Files*. And among exes, life is rarely a cabaret. Grace was no exception to this rule. Her life was...well, fiery. She married dysfunction and she practiced dysfunction. But oh, how she loved those kids.

Grace (portrayed by the talented but tempestuous and self-destructive Brett Butler) was designed by mega-producers Marcy Carsey and Tom Werner—who created *The Cosby Show* and *Roseanne*,

job and raising three growing, needy children. That trio included eight-year-old ruffian Quentin (Jon Paul Steuer and later Sam Horrigan), five-year-old sweetie Libby (Kaitlin Cullum), and baby Patrick (identical twins Dylan and Cole Sprouse).

A fourth kid, Matthew (Tom Everett Scott), would materialize later as the troubled son Grace had given up for adoption at age fifteen. He was now in and out of jail, heaping more trauma onto Grace's broad shoulders. Only her best friends Nadine (Julie White) and Nadine's husband Wade (Casey Sander), along with a low-key pharmacist named Russell (Dave Thomas), could keep Grace from packing it in.

among others—to be an even more rough-hewn version of Roseanne. Her collar was blue, her neck was red, and her instincts in picking men were forever green.

As *Grace Under Fire* debuted, Grace had recently split from her boozing, abusive husband Jimmy (Geoff Pierson) after eight years of marriage, and was determined to make a go of it on her own. Despite her fierce independence and fighting spirit, Grace's situation was complicated by her modest income from an oil refinery

Grace's life was an incessant, chaotic drumbeat of rebuffing men's advances, grappling with her passive-aggressive ex, and struggling to keep Quentin, Libby, and Patrick from growing up too fast (generally without success). But oh, how Grace Kelly tried with her kids. She may have been just a wisecracking trailer-park survivor fighting a slew of demons, but she rarely allowed her offspring to see her sweat.

172

Brett Butler—the onetime battered wife who gave life to Grace—was another story entirely. By all accounts, she turned positively tyrannical on the *Grace Under Fire* set, experiencing frightful anxiety attacks and taking forced sabbaticals until finally ABC had to pull the plug.

If Butler never had her act entirely together, at least Grace worked hard to make it seem as if she did. We can ask little more of our TV moms than that.

Classic Mom-ents

Grace is concerned that her eight-year-old handful of a son, Quentin, is growing up hostile and troubled like his daddy Jimmy. So Grace meets with a child psychologist to discuss her eldest son's conflicted and rebellious nature that leads him to act out his anger at home and at school. Mom and son finally connect during an honest talk.

When Matthew, the son Grace had given up for adoption when she was a teenager, comes back into her life after getting himself in trouble, Grace tracks down the boy's father, Jack. She tells the unaware Jack about Matthew for the first time, but he has no interest in cultivating a relationship with the boy—until the two accidentally meet.

When Grace is beset by money problems and has trouble supporting her three natural kids, Quentin is forced to begin eating free school meals. He asks Grace's boyfriend Rick (Alan Autry) for money, and Rick agrees. At the same time, daughter Libby comes down with a stress ulcer. Grace is overwhelmed by the anxiety she feels she's causing her kids. She is finally able to turn down the anxiety level by opening up the lines of communication—so the kids don't feel responsible to do everything for themselves.

Grace is made to think harder about just what the term "best interests of the child" means, determined to avoid squelching Quentin's wish to live with his father. But her low opinion of her ex invariably overwhelms her judgement and she fights in court to retain primary custody, finally believing that her incessant money problems do not make her a less fit parent—so long as the love and devotion are there.

Left without adequate daytime care for baby son Patrick, Grace defiantly begins a petition drive at her oil refinery job to force the company into opening a day care center on the premises. She is willing to sacrifice her job in the fight.

"I'm tired of trying to do what's fair. I'm tired of being decent and right. It's time for a lawyer."
—Grace Kelly

Cybill Sheridan *(Cybill Shepherd)*

Cybill
(Jan. 2, 1995 to July 13, 1998), CBS

There were a lot of things to love about *Cybill*. One was the wicked and wonderfully bitchy performance by Broadway-trained Christine Baranski as the cynical, well-heeled, deliciously cruel divorcée Maryann. It was a boozy and floozy role that earned Baranski an Emmy. Another winning aspect of the show was its depiction of an ex-husband (named Ira, played by Alan Rosenberg) as a pretty OK guy. The idea that an ex could be decent and cool was a new concept.

But of course, *Cybill* would have been nothing without Cybill Sheridan herself—portrayed with great swagger and self-deprecating gusto by Cybill Shepherd. Cybill was perhaps the first woman in the annals of telemothering who not only didn't run away from the issue of aging, she embraced it and made it the central focus of the show.

It proved to be a canny bit of art imitating life. Here we had Cybill Shepherd, a onetime sex goddess facing middle age and the sobering realities that come with being a working actress in her mid-forties, playing an actress in her mid-forties who was finding the pickings slimmer and slimmer as she aged.

But in the entertainment industry, where a woman's age is a more zealously guarded secret than even her weight or

174

health history, Shepherd insisted that this show tackle the issue of her accumulated years. She did interviews proclaiming how she was ready to be a grandma, and opened doors to help women embrace menopause rather than fear it.

That same defiant feeling permeated *Cybill* itself, which depicted the semi-fictitious Cybill Sheridan as a twice-divorced, semi-embittered, wisecracking actress and mother of two daughters: the adult Rachel (Dedee Pfeiffer) from her first marriage and sixteen-year-old firecracker Zoey (Alicia Witt) from her second. Cybill would become a grandmother before the first season wrapped.

So was Cybill a good mother? Well, let's just say that she was about as solid and centered a mom as any self-centered and neurotic basket case could be. She was there to help mediate her girls' various couplings and uncouplings with boys and men. And she did her best not to belittle their dad too badly.

Yet as Cybill adapted her social skills in order to blend with that princess of pithy patter herself—Maryann—depth turned out not to be Cybill's strong suit. And that's quite OK. Because kids need a TV mother who doesn't waste energy creating facades. They need someone who is, at the very least, legitimate. And that Cybill was—dysfunction and all.

Classic Mom-ents

🕴 Cybill is nearly killed while on the set of an acting gig when a studio light falls and almost crushes her. It inspires her to re-evaluate her priorities and leads to Cybill's deciding to get back together with one of her ex-husbands, Ira. Their sixteen-year-old daughter, Zoey, is quietly thrilled that her parents are reuniting. But since so much is riding on this, best friend Maryann insists on negotiating the terms of their dating. Cybill and her ex don't agree. The reconciliation is off, leaving Zoey to wonder how she is already more mature than her own mother.

🕴 It occurs to Cybill that everybody else has a good life, while her life sucks (or so it appears to her). So Maryann lends Cybill her gold credit card for a shopping spree, which leads to a meditation exercise in the desert to help Cybill find a life's purpose. She locates it hours later when daughter Rachel gives birth and she lays eyes on her first grandchild.

🕴 Rachel asks her mother to attend a marriage counselor with her and her husband, Jeff. But Cybill and Rachel soon discover that Jeff once slept with the counselor. After younger daughter Zoey responds to breaking up with her boyfriend by destroying everything in the house that reminds her of him, Cybill decides to take her girls to a spiritual retreat.

🕴 Cybill is shocked to see her picture on the cover of a porn video box. She lodges a complaint but finally decides that the best revenge would be for her to write her own X-rated movie for women. When she e-mails the script, she accidentally opens Zoey's diary from her trip to Europe and learns how her daughter lost her virginity. Cybill confronts Zoey, who is deeply hurt that her mother would look through her private book. Then she insists it's all fantasy.

When Rachel suspects her husband Kevin of having an affair, it's left to Cybill to talk her daughter out of having her own affair in retaliation. While the two of them are out together, they see Zoey's boyfriend Sean dating another girl behind Zoey's back. Cybill briefly wrestles with the dilemma of whether or not to tell her daughter.

"For your information, Miss Smarty Pants, the producer of the Julie! show loves me and wants me back tomorrow. And once and for all, Grover set himself on fire. But does anyone believe me? Nooooo! Because Muppets don't lie!"
—Cybill

Debra Barone (Patricia Heaton) and *Marie Barone* (Doris Roberts)

Everybody Loves Raymond
(Sept. 13, 1996 to present), CBS

Yes, everybody loves Raymond. And everybody drives him crazy, too. That's the premise of this genuinely funny and clever family comedy that stars stand-up comedian Ray Romano as Ray Barone, an affable New York sportswriter with a high-energy wife, a high-maintenance mother, a very tall and insecure doofus of an older brother, and three fairly nondescript kids. It has become essential viewing to hang out with such a winningly befuddled everyman and the winningly neurotic moms in his orbit.

Those women would be Ray's wife Debra Barone (played with spunk by Patricia Heaton) and his meddling mother Marie (scene-stealing work by Doris Roberts). Because of Marie, Ray and Debra are literally without privacy. Marie lives across the street from them and has been known to drop by unannounced and even raid the couple's fridge along with Ray's quirky dad Frank (the incomparable Peter Boyle).

While the smothering Marie invades the space of her son and daughter-in-law, Ray and Debra do everything possible to avoid her. Nothing works. And Ray gets no sympathy from his policeman brother (comedian Brad Garrett), who maintains everyone loves Raymond more than they love him.

Debra, a full-time mother, is a scrapper and a wisecracker of great intensity who believes Ray could do a lot more to keep his mom out of their lives. He agrees and then does nothing. Debra will demean her husband without a second thought but saves her real venom for Marie. Their catfights are scenes to behold: great bursts of sarcasm and venom that set the synapses on overdrive.

As the stay-at-home mom with an attitude and a smart mouth, Debra is all about defending her turf. If she doesn't do all that much real mothering of her children, it's OK, because each new day means going several more rounds in the wrestling match that is her life.

Marie seems to be biding her time, figuring that if she sticks it out long enough she will break the spirit of Debra as she has for Ray. She is like a child who is unable to accept any form of rejection, and she's trained her sons well. They understand that mother cannot be defied, only humored. She can't be controlled, merely temporarily contained. She feels it her right to live her sons' life as well as her own, and that's that.

Together, Debra and Marie are quite the pair. And as such, they are a genuine inspiration for the next generation of telemothers.

Classic Mom-ents

♀ Debra decides, after years of her mother-in-law Marie's cooking the traditional Thanksgiving Day dinner, that it is now her turn. But not wanting to compete with Marie's mouthwatering turkey, Debra cooks fish instead. Marie freaks out and brings her own turkey along.

♀ Sick of reading her young daughter Ally the same stories night after night, Debra makes plans to try her hand at writing a children's book. She feels empowered to be doing something other than being a housewife, and invites husband Raymond to write the story with her. But when his ego gets in the way, Ray turns their little project into a full-blown competition. It would prove to be a big mistake to challenge his wife on what she perceives to be her telemothering turf.

♀ After Marie drops in on her Tupperware party and empties the room with her rudeness, Debra writes her mother-in-law an irate letter demanding that Marie quit intruding in her life. Ray fears that once his mother reads the letter, their lives will spontaneously end. But surprisingly, the honesty strikes a cord.

♀ At Ally's T-ball game, Debra begins to lose respect for Raymond when her Mr. Nice Guy hubby fails to stick up for their daughter in the face of a pushy parent with whom Debra has just had a run-in. In Debra's mind, this is a clear-cut issue of protecting your kid in the face of adversity. Her husband sees it quite differently—and they wind up having to agree to disagree.

♀ Marie feels insulted when Debra hires another babysitter rather than asking her to sit. So Debra dismisses the sitter halfway through the night and tells Marie to come on over. Quickly, Marie discovers that she lacks the energy to keep up with the kids and finally trips over a toy and injures herself.

Debra: I was planning our wedding since I was twelve years old. . . . You were just the last piece of the puzzle.

Marie: Bobby, get your father his helping of Miserable Bastard.

179

Annie Camden
(Catherine Hicks)

7th Heaven
(Aug. 27, 1996 to present), The WB

Now this is one interesting mother, just as *7th Heaven* is one underestimated drama series. For one, it is created and executive produced by Aaron Spelling, who is known more for nighttime soaps and sizzle than for this type of quality work—though he has had others, including the Emmy-winning HBO film *And the Band Played On*. It is also something of a new millennium hybrid in that it carries 1950s values in a contemporary package.

Annie Camden (Catherine Hicks), for example, is a model wife and mother of seven kids, the youngest being twin babies David and Samuel. She is a full-time stay-at-home mom whose husband is the Reverend Eric Camden (Stephen Collins). So we have a housewife and a minister living with their bigger-than-Brady brood in the suburbs of Los Angeles.

Sounds pretty sedate and a little like *Little House on the Prairie*, doesn't it? Sure it does. But it's actually not even close. While *7th Heaven* has its moral compass and its traditional beliefs rooted in the '50s, it's got enough crises to keep its youthful target audience riveted like glue.

Annie is one strong and independent lady, dispensing tough love and kindheartedness in equal doses. She also diverts from the telemothering ideal in that she serves as her household's handyman, so to speak, not only doing the cooking but laying electrical wire, fixing the plumbing, and performing carpentry as if it were second nature.

But it's quite frankly a good thing that Annie is such a domestic dynamo and has everything so together, considering the chronic dysfunction, upheaval and trauma that orbit around she and her tight-knit, loving family. In just three and a half years, the Camdens have encountered teen pregnancy, racial and ethnic prejudice, drug abuse, spousal abuse, alcoholism, assault, cancer, and various moral dilemmas—and not a single household member has flipped out.

That home features seventeen-year-old son Matt (Barry Watson), fifteen-year-old Mary (Jessica Biel), thirteen-year-old Lucy (Beverley Mitchell), eleven-year-old Simon (David Gallagher), and six-year-old Ruthie Camden (Mackenzie Rosman) as well as the twins and, oh yes, a dog named Happy. The kids all find themselves in various stages of hormone detonation and puberty adjustment.

To handle it all with such grace and skill, Annie has to be June Cleaver, Carol Brady, Roseanne Conner, and Arnold

Schwarzenegger rolled into one. That she is. The kids all manage to get individual nurturing despite Annie's obvious preoccupation with infant twins. It could only happen on TV. That's what makes it so much fun.

Classic Mom-ents

♀ Annie gives birth to twins David and Samuel on Valentine's Day, which brings her and husband Eric's number of children to seven. At the hospital, their parents and five other kids continue a tradition that began with child number one: they all serenade her with the Mary Tyler Moore Show theme song ("You're gonna make it after all…"). Of course, that tune originally referred to an unmarried woman with no kids.

♀ When Annie's parents spend the weekend at her home, she awakens with a vision of her mother telling her how much she loves her but admitting, "It's time to go." Annie rushes to her mother's room to find her dead. The devastating premonition leaves her absorbed with the relationship she has with her own kids and vows never to take it for granted again.

♀ Annie and son Matt are held up at gunpoint while pulled off to the side of the road with car trouble. The criminal demands their money and jewelry, taking Annie's wedding rings as well. Afterward, Annie realizes how close one of her children came to being killed, and it causes her to lose her trust in people.

♀ Fighting an addiction to alcohol, Julie—Annie's sister—attacks her nephew Simon when he tries to keep the key to the family liquor cabinet away from her. Annie luckily walks in as the ugly incident is unfolding and forcefully removes her sister from the house as Simon cowers nearby.

♀ Matt's parents accuse him of smoking marijuana when they find a joint on the floor near his jacket pocket. He is mortified at the charge and runs, shaken up badly, to church to pray aloud. It turns out that he was given the joint by a friend and didn't know what to do with it. Annie and Eric apologize profusely.

"If you run away from everything that scares you, you're going to miss out on a lot of good stuff in life."
—Annie Camden

Peggy Hill
(*Kathy Najimy*)

King of the Hill
(Jan. 12, 1996 to present), Fox

It isn't easy being a substitute Spanish teacher in the middle of redneck country, and Peggy Hill—who lives with her animated family in the suburban, beer-swilling paradise that is Arlen, Texas—shows the battle scars of trying to teach a foreign language while she's struggling to be the best wife and mother she can be.

Then again, the bespectacled, somewhat frumpy Peggy (voiced by Kathy Najimy) is not really one to ask for a tremendous amount out of life. Her favorite author is Nolan Ryan. Her proudest achievement is having earned the title of Texas State Boggle Champion. But let it be said that Peg Hill is nobody's fool and is, indeed, one tough woman, to the great frustration of her hubby, Hank (the voice of creator-producer Mike Judge).

Peg's tendency to take no one's nonsense likewise makes childhood more of a challenge for her twelve-year-old son Bobby (Pamela Segall Adlon), a chubby, carrot-topped lad who is awkward, timid, and (worst of all in Texas) disinterested in football. In fact, Bobby is something of an anti-jock. He has no aptitude for sports, or actually for much of anything else, either.

And so like any neurotic TV mom, Peggy Hill worries that her son will never amount to anything. This concern is lent further merit by Hank's status as Bobby's prime role model. Hank is forty, a propane

Bill (Stephen Root), a divorced slob who wears tank T-shirts and sips suds with abandon; and Boomhauer (Judge), whose drawl is so heavy it sounds as if he speaks through molasses.

Peggy does her level best to deal sensibly with all of the senselessness in her midst. She keeps Bobby on a short leash because if he wandered too far, he might just lay down and call it a life. She also keeps a vigilant eye peeled on her loosely-moraled, dim-witted niece Luanne (Brittany Murphy) who lives with the Hills and is extremely gullible.

Somehow, Peg does the telemothering community proud with her devotion, her decency, and her straitlaced, heavy-handed form of tough love. Behind those specs lives a mom who luckily doesn't yet realize just how heavily the odds are stacked against her. The sincere hope is that she never will.

gas salesman with ultra-conservative values who sees country hoedowns as high culture. He hangs out with three pals of equally limited focus: Dale (Johnny Hardwick), who sees everything as a conspiracy of some sort;

Classic Mom-ents

♀ Peggy Hill's well-meaning husband Hank is accused of child abuse when he throws a temper tantrum at their twelve-year-old son Bobby in a hardware store just an hour or so after Bobby received a black eye while playing baseball. But Peggy defends her husband to an intense social worker that her husband is as gentle as a lamb and was incapable of such a thing. Hank promises to better control his temper.

♀ When a note from school requests Bobby's participation in a sexual education class, Hank hits the roof and volunteers Peggy to do the honors instead. A death threat to the regular teacher results in Peg's teaching Bobby's entire class. Hank ultimately realizes how courageous his wife is to utter words such as "vagina" aloud.

♀ Hank learns that his shapely young niece Luanne—who lives with him, Peggy, and Bobby—owes six months in back rent for the trailer she abandoned at a nearby trailer park. He is furious and insists that she move out. That brings Peggy to Luanne's rescue. She calls Hank an emotionless "blockhead" and storms off with Luanne. A tornado destroys Luanne's trailer, and Peg insists that Luanne remain with the Hills.

♀ Peggy loses her job as a substitute teacher after spanking an unruly student who had pulled down her pants in front of the class. A petition is promptly circulated demanding Peggy's reinstatement. She wins back her job but returns to class carrying a huge paddle. Bobby freaks out over his mother's sudden aggressiveness, which has won her the nickname Paddlin' Peggy.

♀ After Bobby abuses his responsibility and allows a seedy party to be thrown in a house he is watching for vacationing neighbors, he and Luanne begin to feud. They pull mean-spirited pranks on one another, including one where Bobby replaces Luanne's birth control pills with candy. Peggy is irate with Bobby, and she and Hank order him to do the only right thing: marry her. They actually hold a mock ceremony for the pair until finally Peggy decides the boy has learned his lesson well enough.

"You cannot make authentic guacamole out of lima beans and Ritz crackers."
—Peggy Hill

Eric Cartman's Mom *(Shannen Cassidy)*
South Park
(Aug. 13, 1997 to present), Comedy Central

Mrs. Cartman—unmarried mother of squat, blubbery, foul-mouthed Eric Cartman—may just be the most twisted character on the most twisted animated series in television history because she takes such pains to try and appear wholesome. She dresses like a schoolmarm, speaks like an innocent, and appears to spend much of her time baking brownies and tidying up the house she shares with her repugnant and ill-tempered lad.

Yet at the same time, Mrs. Cartman, who has never been given a first name by *South Park* co-creators Matt Stone and Trey Parker, has a decidedly wild streak. She has, for instance, donned the cover of Crack Whore magazine. She is also said to have slept with every person—man, woman, and child—in the entire town, according to oddball schoolteacher Mr. Garrison.

So if you're keeping score, this would mean that Mrs. Cartman is something of a two-sided fraud: pure of speech, devoted mom, crack user, alcoholic, and slut. Yet we have to love this woman because she's wholly endearing as she puts so much effort toward maintaining her misleading façade.

And of course, this odd combination of traits for a cartoon character is very much in holding with the eccentric and racy style that has defined *South Park* since it first exploded onto the cable TV scene in August 1997. It

was a cult hit and an Internet smash even before it arrived on television thanks to a much-distributed video Christmas card that bootlegged its way around the country. (The seven-minute short found the cursing *South Park* kiddie gang serving as spectators of a battle between Jesus Christ and Santa Claus over the true meaning of Christmas.)

That offbeat, savage precursor set the tone for a series that quickly became the most talked about new show of 1997 and has since spawned a hit feature film, *South Park: Bigger, Longer and Uncut*. And it produced the tramp of all TV moms, Mrs. Cartman (voiced by Shannen Cassidy, who tragically committed suicide in November 1999).

Besides her boozing, drugging, and whoring secret life, Mrs. Cartman is also a pretty lousy mother, though a particularly colorful one. She allows Eric to boss her around and do as he pleases, simultaneously encouraging his weight problem by feeding him a diet of ham, chocolate chicken pot pie, Cheesy Poofs, and Snaky Cakes. She also carried with her a longtime secret: she was born with both male and female reproductive organs and did not, in point of fact, give birth to her son; rather, she fathered him.

Confused yet? It's all part of the *South Park* charm—and the entertaining ambiguity of a mother who could use a little mothering herself.

Classic Mom-ents

- Mrs. Cartman admits to son Eric that she in fact has no idea who his father is, since he was conceived at the twelfth annual Drunken Barn Dance. Her last memory is of being with a fellow named Chief Running Water. But when confronted, Eric's teacher Mr. Garrison says that his mother has "been with" everyone in town, including the entire 1989 Denver Broncos team.

- The character Mephesto announces that a DNA test reveals Mrs. Cartman to in fact be a hermaphrodite who cannot bear children, meaning she is technically Eric Cartman's father rather than his mother.

- Mrs. Cartman is concerned that Eric's attending the taping of a certain TV show will inspire him to acquire "a potty mouth," but Eric sets her straight by replying, "Screw off, Mom!" Her reply: "Oh, OK, hon."

- When son Eric decides to dress up as Adolf Hitler for Halloween, Mrs. Cartman offers, "Dear, you look so dangerous!" Eric would later switch to a slightly less offensive Ku Klux Klan costume.

- Mrs. Cartman bakes chocolate chicken pot pies for Eric and all of his friends, though Eric would consume many of his friends' pies as well.

"But dear, you're not fat. You're big-boned!"
—Mrs. Cartman

Livia Soprano (Nancy Marchand)
and *Carmela Soprano* (Edie Falco)

The Sopranos
(Jan. 10, 1999 to present), HBO

It is hard to imagine that television could stride further away from its sweetness-and-light TV mom roots than Livia and Carmela Soprano, the ladies who pour considerable dysfunctional fuel on the fire that is the extraordinary HBO series *The Sopranos*.

Consider that Livia (the superb Nancy Marchand) is the seventy-year-old widow of Johnny Boy Soprano and the mother of modern-day New Jersey Mob capo Tony Soprano and his two sisters. Since Johnny Boy's death, she has lived alone, in complete isolation, losing her marbles in increasingly large numbers. As the first season of *The Sopranos* came to an end in 1999, Livia had just ordered a "hit" on Tony. Hey, it's just business.

Then there is Carmela Soprano, the role for which Edie Falco earned a 1999 Emmy award. Carmela is Tony's long-suffering wife of eighteen years. She has put up with the assassinations, the mistresses (or "goomahs" in mob parlance), and the decrepit fathering skills. Now, she is being asked to accept that her husband may be the most emotionally unbalanced thug on the East Coast, and that he is in therapy with a doctor who is also a beautiful woman (Lorraine Bracco).

Yes, while Tony Soprano suffers panic attacks and struggles to get in touch with his inner mobster, Carmela gets the shaft. And she don't like it one little bit. She knows that her husband hurts people and breaks all sorts of laws for a living, but what can she do? She can't trade Tony in for a sleeker and sturdier model. And so Carmela suffers.

But even mob wives have their limits, and it appears as if the bright, saucy Carmela's line in the sand surrounds the safety of her sixteen-year-old daughter, honor student Meadow (Jamie Lynn Sigler), and fourteen-year-old video game addict Anthony Jr. (Robert Iler). During the first season of *The Sopranos*, it was looking as if Tony's enemies might hurt the family if he wasn't careful. Worse, Anthony Jr. had begun to fancy himself a street tough. Carmela remains, however, a defiant mother hen with no real power.

Livia, meanwhile, is nothing less than a telemom for the ages. She gripes at Tony incessantly about his life, his wife, her neighbors, her water pipes, the heat, the cold—the list is endless. And when her anger is ignored, it turns surrealistically nasty. She clearly raised Tony with a silver gun muzzle in his mouth.

Anyone who has watched *The Sopranos* understands that it reaches the level of true art as a darkly comic mob opera, one that is alternately grim and utterly eccentric. And Livia and Carmela are two big reasons why it all works so well. They are the very essence of neurosis-driven anguish—and we love them to death for it.

Classic Mom-ents

⚦ Carmela is called in to speak with the principal at her son Anthony Jr.'s Catholic school. She's told that he and his posse stole sacramental wine and showed up to gym class drunk. Carmela punishes her son by taking away his sacred Nintendo console and forcing him to do good deeds such as visiting his grandmother at her retirement community. It is while talking with her grandson that Livia discovers her son Tony is in therapy.

⚦ Livia is so incensed that Tony is seeing a therapist—concerned that he may be spilling family secrets to a shrink—that she begins to tell everyone she knows in the mobster community, to put his life in jeopardy. She even schemes with Tony's uncle, Junior (who is equally concerned) to "whack" her son in order to shut him up. When the hit is unsuccessful, Livia conveniently begins to forget things, fails to recognize her own granddaughter, and apparently suffers a stroke.

⚦ Livia insists that she can take care of herself. She refuses Tony's pleadings to place her in New Jersey's best retirement community, Green Grove. "Why don't you stab me in the heart, right here!" Livia wails to her son, preferring death to being forced out of her home.

⚲ Following the unsuccessful attempt on Tony's life, an FBI agent approaches Tony and wife Carmela about "rolling over" on his mob buddies. Carmela appeals to Tony that they all consider entering the federal witness protection program for the sake of the kids. "They need a father," she insists. "They got one!" Tony replies. "Tony Soprano. And all that comes with it."

⚲ Carmela shares a cherished yearly ritual with her daughter Meadow: a trip to the Plaza in New York City for tea and shopping. But when Carmela punishes Meadow for sneaking out of the house at night by forbidding her to go on a ski trip with her friends, Meadow snipes to her mom that she's never liked going to the Plaza with her at all.

"All day she runs the water. Water, water, water. I'm living next door to Gunga Din!"
—Livia

"What are you, a kid in a treehouse?"
—Carmela

190

Acknowledgments

While compiling the mother of all television books was in many respects a labor of love, it could not have come together without the peerless contributions of numerous individuals and research tools.

At the head of those lists are Tim Brooks and the reference guide he co-authored, *The Complete Directory to Prime Time Network and Cable TV Shows (Twentieth Anniversary Edition)*. It is, quite simply, the ultimate television resource, representing 1,363 pages of uncanny historical perspective and insight. The book proved invaluable, as did the tireless Brooks himself.

The World Wide Web stood out as a second indispensible study guide and information clearinghouse. It continues to astonish that there are so many fans of TV in cyberspace who take the time to pay tribute to classic shows from the tube's past with reverent, often wonderfully entertaining fan-sites. A particular debt of thanks goes out to David Tanny, curator of the *Eight Is Enough* Fan/Info Page, for his terrific assistance on short notice.

While *TV Moms* was produced entirely without the aid of any of the moms themselves, the bright and scrappy Paul Peterson came through with superior memories of his telemom Donna Reed on *The Donna Reed Show*. He is a true gentleman and a scholar who has left Hollywood a better place than he found it.

My gratitude also goes out to TV's sassy Nick at Nite for keeping the TV mom fires burning all these years; to my TV Books editor Albert DePetrillo, whose uncommon patience and wisdom helped make these pages a whole lot better; and to the mothers of television themselves, who have done more to set the maternal tone in society than is commonly recognized.

I also take the opportunity to thank my own mother, Terri Richmond, a marvelously eccentric soul who makes Roseanne Conner look like Betty Crocker. And I'm grateful to have such sincere and nurturing mothers-in-law in Dorothy Abramson and Linda Lieberman. Lastly, I offer my most passionate admiration for my wife, Heidi, whose unmatched skills as a mother provided inspiration throughout the construction of this book. I hope our son Dylan understands how lucky he is.

—Ray Richmond